Success is a Verb!

Success is a Verb!
Making every day a success
with the power of
Habit Replacement Therapy

Second Edition
Revised and Expanded

Rick Berube
with
Tracie K Petras

Published by Rick Berube
Las Vegas, Nevada

Dedicated to
Jacqueline Berube, and William and Margaret Dufoe.
Without them, this book would not have been possible.
To Tina Phyfer,
For pushing me to the finish line.
And to my four spectacular kids,
Nicolas, Derek, Willow, and Bodhi.
I hope they will decide to use some of the ideas herein
(but you know how kids listen!)

Contents

INTRODUCTION

We are what we repeatedly do.
Excellence, then, is not an act but a habit.
—Aristotle

More than thirteen hundred years ago, Aristotle had already figured out that habits play a significant role in shaping human character. He also knew (as we do today), that habits are learned, being the outcome of thoughts and actions repeated often enough that we can perform these actions with little effort or thought. Indeed, some habits are so firmly rooted that we don't even know we have them. Take them away, however, and we would be so overwhelmed by the decisions and tasks needed to survive, that we would have little time left to ponder the world or chase down a dream.

Fortunately, we are creatures of habit. I have no doubt that our habits have been with us at least as far back in our history as the beginning of agriculture some 12,000 years ago. In terms of physical and cultural evolution, the effect of this shift to agriculture has been nothing less than profound (Diamond, 2006). As our distant ancestors made the transition from nomadic hunter-gatherers to living in settled communities as farmers and herders, more time would have become available to take advantage of what must have been a natural curiosity in the world.

Humans possess a seemingly infinite capacity to learn and an extraordinary ability to imagine ourselves in the future. This enables us to anticipate and plan for events in order to effect the outcome—for things that haven't even happened yet. This is a remarkable human feature rarely found in nature, and it will play a central role throughout our history. Planning and effecting the future has led us to become masters of adaptation. It was an easy leap from there to the top of the food chain and the belief that we are masters of the Earth. I wonder though, are we equally masters of our own behavior?

Not always. We often struggle against learning anything that takes effort, and change of all sorts can be downright threatening. (If you were among the casualties of the sweeping corporate layoffs during the 1980s, you know the fear of change.) Every time we set our minds to the task of learning a new skill or a new routine, we have to make a change in our behavior—and we all know what that kind of change is: it's hard! In fact, we've managed to convince ourselves that we cannot change how we are and that this condition is normal. We've even gone so far as to force the idea on our pets. You can't teach an old dog new tricks, after all. Well, yes, you can. But it's hard.

Now you know the downside to habit change. But we can change and we can learn new behaviors. Any thought or action is able to become a habit, but it has to be learned through practice that can be difficult and time consuming. Think about driving a car, for example. Ideally, before getting behind the wheel we have to learn the rules of the road and pass a written test to verify our knowledge. Then, from the driver's seat, we have to watch our speed, stay within the lines, check our blind spot, and keep our eyes on the road and on everything else around us in every direction and all at the same time; we have to pay attention to the gauges and meters on the dash board, comply with all the traffic signs and signals, and anticipate what the other guy will do next; we use our hands to steer and to shift gears, and we apply the clutch and hit the brakes with our feet ... while simultaneously making split-second decisions based on all this sensory data we've been taking in. With practice, our ability to process the incoming flood of detail becomes second nature while driving becomes just another habit. This is the beauty where it all comes together. Habit is what makes it possible to merge a car safely onto the freeway and drive at speeds in excess of 55 miles per hour while singing along to Madonna's *Like a Virgin*. The fact is, we go about our daily lives while our habits run silently in the background, largely unnoticed. Silently, that is, until we acquire a bad one.

You know what they are. Smoking. Overeating. Alcohol abuse. I am sure you can come up with a few more. These habits of addiction wreak havoc on the lives of the afflicted and disrupt the lives of family and friends. Addictive behavior is extremely difficult to overcome, especially substance abuse that usually requires outside support or intervention and a struggle for sobriety that goes on for years—if not for an entire lifetime. These bad habits can kill.

There is another bad sort of behavior that is not easily recognized because when this behavior occurs in an isolated incident (versus something done repeatedly), it is noticed and forgotten quickly. Only when it reaches the regularity of a habit does this behavior become a problem. Let's say I get to work late one morning but I have a history of on-time performance. The infraction is a first so I am forgiven. But what if I make it a habit? It is highly unlikely that habitual tardiness will kill me, but going hungry after being fired is not a good situation for me. When any pattern of behavior or thought keeps you from achieving your goals or stands in the way of your ability to meet obligations and responsibilities, then your routine is a bad habit that limits your life choices and what you can achieve. The life you want and deserve will remain just out of reach.

My goal is to give you a powerful set of tools and ideas that can transform your life. The methods in this book are so simple to use and easy to understand that you can start using them *today*. I call this method habit replacement therapy, the process of getting rid of old routines that are holding you back by replacing them with positive habits designed to encourage you to achieve your goals, and ultimately, to allow you to live the life of your dreams.

The Joy in the Journey!
There is a lot of work to do. Just when you think you have put in enough, you get tested again. You might doubt your abilities or question why

you chose a new path. You have to believe the joy is in the journey! It is so important that you love what you do. Of course, there might be occasional moments of frustration that overshadow the good, but I am talking about the big picture here. You have to love and value your career. I think Steve Jobs said it best during an interview on YouTube. "You have to love what you do almost to the point of obsession because it's going to take a lot of work and you'll be tested on the way."

Let's face it, average, sane people occasionally throw up their hands in despair while declaring, "Okay, enough already!" Insanely successful people are known to do the same thing but with one critical difference. Successful people will keep at it even with the pain of failure and after the average person has long given up. The path to success makes you a little bit loony, or maybe you have to be a little bit crazy to reach for it in the first place. Either way, successful people are just different. But then, Henry Ford and Thomas Edison would probably say that this is not such a bad thing.

Failure Done Right
Highly successful people are experts in failure. If we knew their ratio of successes to failures, I

think we would be surprised by how often the successful fail. It's not that high achievers are equipped with magical super-human talent. When they fail, chances are they have the same feelings of frustration as the rest of us do. The difference is that failure for highly successful people is not reason enough for them to give up on their goals.

It's all in the attitude. You can change your attitude towards failure and frustration so that instead of a reason to give up, a disappointing outcome is an opportunity to re-evaluate your actions. Use the energy you would have otherwise wasted on frustration, for a constructive purpose that supports your goals.

Nearly everything in life worth having will require a measure of work. We value the product of our labor more than that which comes easily to us because we are engaged in the process that leads to the reward; we know in real terms what it takes to get what we want. You will have to develop self-discipline if this is a weakness for you. Again, the choice is yours whether to make the necessary changes or to accept things as they are and do nothing.

Failure should not determine your success. You can break the link between frustration and quitting by changing your point of view. From now on, think of frustration as merely a warning that it is time to increase your efforts or reconsider your strategy. If your energy is drained, allow yourself some down time, and then start again.

How to Make this Book Work for You

This book is intended to be a guide for building a positive future and to help you achieve *your* success in whatever endeavor you choose. Improve your golf game, sail the Pacific, land a promotion, or find an end to world hunger. Or get rich. Use this book as a concise resource you can carry in your pocket or purse to find quick inspiration, ideas, and reminders that point you in the right direction for help if you should get stuck.

The desire to overcome a bad habit is something that every one of us will face eventually. There is no shortage of self-help models out there, so many that choosing one is itself a chore. Who has time? It looked to me like some clarity was needed so I gathered the best of what works combined with my own insights from years of experience coaching and training others. Each chapter is organized around a different theme and each successive chapter builds on the one before. Although meant to be read straight through from beginning to end, each chapter can be read independently to fit your needs and goals. There is no right or wrong to it.

I have been through most of what I write about. My words are based on experience and come from the heart. Over the years, through personal struggles and as a coach helping others achieve what they want in their lives, I have learned first hand what works and what does not. It is my sincere hope that within these pages you will find something that works for you.

Please let me know how you are doing. Ask questions. Stay open to the future and think in terms of positive action. When your actions are positive, they strengthen the belief in your potential. Know that you have the power to change. Tap into that power and you will transform your life!

SUCCESS

Quit now. You'll never make it.
If you disregard this advice,
you'll be halfway there.
—David Zucker

Like it or not, the measure of our lives is made by success. We are constantly being told what success is, whether or not we have it, and the awful consequences of failing to achieve enough of it. The result is our tendency to judge the success of others, not by their deeds and achievements, but by the car they drive, the house they live in, and whether their bath towels have a certain bouncy fresh softness.

According to the fourth edition of Webster's New World College Dictionary success can be 1) a favorable outcome; 2) a person who has achieved a degree of rank, fame, or money; or 3) the prosperous termination of an endeavor or the accomplishment of one's goals (Agnes, 2010). Like desert after dinner, you attain success only when you are done.

Most of us would probably agree with the dictionary, of course, and there is nothing wrong with leaving it at that. However, why not take the point of view that success is an active part of a fulfilled life rather than its final reward? Why not take control of your own success instead of letting someone else make decisions for you?

In this way, success will vary depending on a person's values and priorities. You will measure it differently than I do but both of us will base our decisions on a combination of three factors: things that are specifically important to us as individuals, what our chosen goals are, and the standards in common by the people we spend the most time with.

I want to challenge your usual way of thinking. Instead of success standing for the end of something, widen your field of view. Picture success as a springboard for action or a habit for living; as a reason to get up every morning and head out for the day on a non-stop collision course towards your goals; success is the spark that moves you forward even during those days when you don't really feel like it, and then, when your dreams are so close you can reach out and touch them ... success is the engine that drives you to set a new goal, higher than the last. This is how you maximize your potential.

Success is a verb! It is a process that evolves with your goals and the habits you create to achieve them. Think about it. Each of us is exactly where we are today because of the choices we have made and the actions we have repeated over time. Each one of us has a unique repertoire of habits and everyday routines—literally hundreds of them—that simplify, regulate, and navigate our lives through a world that continually bombards us with sights, sounds, and choices. This automation is so important that our brains are actually hardwired at birth to be receptive to habit building. Without them, we would simply freeze under the weight of sensory overload.

By far, the majority of our habits are positive, but there always seems to be one or two that do us no good. Too bad, they don't come equipped with a remote on and off switch. In order to change, you are going to have to get up and do it yourself. If you want to make a change that sticks, the kind with a meaningful, positive impact, you are going to have to take responsibility for your behavior, make a commitment to change, and be willing to do the necessary work.

If you are reading this book, you have probably reached a turning point in your life. For any number of reasons, you want to make some changes. You may have been rolling the idea around in your head for a while because things just aren't working out the way you thought they would. Maybe you had a wake up call, an experience with enough impact to snap you out of autopilot—that condition where boredom, stress, or lack of focus can cause you to lose sight of the more important things in life—and you want some help getting back on track. Whatever the reason, you are here now and now is the time to take action.

Habit Replacement Therapy

Okay, I admit the name sounds funny but habit replacement therapy can help you maximize your potential and create a daily routine that will have a positive impact on your life.

How do you maximize your potential? By replacing negative old habits with positive new ones. I know, I know, bad habits—and yes, you *know* they are bad—are notoriously resistant to change. Why? Well, one reason has a lot to do with human biology. Certain habits (like the bad ones—hell, especially the bad ones), are quick to reward you with pleasure. Pleasure is the sensation you feel when the body releases the hormone dopamine into your blood stream. Our brains love dopamine. To get more, we repeat the behavior associated with the release of dopamine and the cycle goes on, repeating itself until a habit is formed. And every time you repeat the behavior, it gets that much harder to stop. It's not your fault; it's that darn biology!

Smoking is the perfect example to illustrate how this process works. If you have ever tried to smoke, you know what happens, all the coughing and gaging with those first puffs on a cigarette. But you are motivated to learn (a cigarette held aloft makes one look oh so smart and well traveled!) so you practice and practice until eventually you can smoke with the best of them. Now you've done it. You have successfully created a very bad habit, one that you cannot seem to stop.

That's the bad news. But there is good news, too. Remember how you had to practice to get in the bad habit of smoking? You can do the same thing to create a positive habit or routine.

If you are anything like me, you know how difficult change can be. Fortunately, our brains are flexible and capable of learning new things even in the face of some pretty tough obstacles. The key is in persistence and practice. If you follow through and keep repeating the new activity, your brain will quickly learn the behavior and commit it to memory. Soon you will have set the foundation for a new, more productive habit.

It has been said that habits make the man. Aristotle proposed the maxim, "We are what we repeatedly do." In other words, if your goal is to be more productive, you need to get in the habit of planning. If you want to be physically fit, you need the habit of exercise. Look at the habits in your life. What do they say about you?

If you want to reduce that restless feeling of being unfocused and replace it with a happier, more productive outlook, it is imperative that you break from your bad habits and develop good ones in their place. For this, you need a plan. If you have to make decisions every single day about whether you are going to go to the gym or read a good book, when you allow those routine choices to be left to the whim of the moment or to the day's circumstances or your current mood, you will spend more time running in circles instead of ahead.

This is just a single point in the daily cycle. There's also the point that it's mentally and physically draining to make the same decisions day after day, and the more you fail to live up to your goals and the more times you break a promise to yourself, the less confident you become and the fewer successes you will have with each new endeavor. Keep up this counter-routine for any length of time and it won't be long until you see yourself as a failure and all of this becomes a miserable habit in a cycle that feeds on a self-fulfilling prophecy.

People who believe that life is hard often feel that way because they have not developed the kind of habits that support a positive, meaningful life. This type of failure can turn every day into a tug of war between what they want to accomplish and what they end up with instead. Lost to them is that sweet spot where habits make them stronger, healthier, and happier, where most of your everyday decisions and behavior have become automatic, freeing your time to focus on what really matters and giving you that feeling so central to a satisfied life: that feeling of making continual progress.

If you are not happy where you are with your habits, you'll find practical tips in every chapter that are simple and effective in turning things around. I know this because I've seen it happen.

One of my main goals when I was in the real estate sales business was to become the most successful salesperson I could be. I'm willing to guess that you want to be the best you can be in your career. I am also willing to take it a step further and tell you that you already have the potential to achieve the level of success you want. The question is, how do you reach that potential?

Over the years, I have seen hundreds of successful people achieve their dreams. I have seen over and over the same characteristics make the best of them stand out from the rest. As it turns out, all habitually successful people seem to have five characteristics in common. The great news is that all five qualities can be learned by anyone with commitment and practice.

The Five Qualities of Success

First, successful people start with the end in mind. Let me explain by giving you an example from real estate sales: "My goal this year is to complete 75 deals. Based on my numbers from last year, I need to make 32 contacts per day. I make 11 contacts per hour, which means I need to prospect three hours a day," and so on throughout their schedule to quantify the entire day. They also use their minds to visualize specific images of what they want and what they have to do to get there. They use photos and pictures to illustrate their goals, which are then posted to a dream board that they see every day. Their dream board is both a reminder of the reward they are working for, and a way to reinforce the "why" in what they do each day. The physical pictures and the mental images together are a powerful incentive. The result is tremendous success.

Second, successful people are fearless. They live by the motto "Feel the fear and do it anyway!" They know it's not always easy to do the work that is necessary to make change happen, but they certainly feel great when it's done! It's not always easy to tell the truth to themselves and to others, but it's the right thing to do. It takes courage to step out of a familiar environment and do something in a new way instead of the comfortable old way they have always done it. Change always involves some degree of risk and any time there is a risk, even an educated one, there is an element of fear. Of course there's fear. Fear helped our ancestors survive long enough to carry their heritage into the future; fear is a signal to act with caution, to use your brain rather than to act blindly. Success is feeling the fear without being frozen by it.

Third, success takes a lot of energy. Successful people seem to have energy in reserve. There will always be those occasional days when they have to fake it to make it, so they have devised certain strategies to keep up their energy level. One of these strategies is having a powerful morning habit: get up early, spend time reading, meditating, praying, or saying affirmations, and then some type of workout routine. This could be anything from a high-intensity weight circuit to a nice long walk, and anything in between. If your morning routine does nothing to boost your energy and give you an attitude to match, it's time to make the switch to full time!

The fourth quality successful people have is their great people skills. Communication is central when it comes to successful relationships, even more so if you are in a sales situation. Even people outside the field of professional sales will find themselves in sales situations on a daily basis. Any time the goal is to convince someone to do or believe something, you are in a sales situation. Parents trying to get their kids to eat more vegetables, a wife convincing an errant husband to take the trash out, and your teenager persuading you that they are mature enough are all examples of selling in everyday life.

An important skill for sales professionals is building rapport. One way to achieve this connection with your clients is to repeat and approve what your client/prospect says while remaining your authentic self. Being able to mirror and match your prospect's communication style and body language takes some practice to master but when you do, you will you stand out from the competition in a good way. For the non-professional, your relationships with others will improve in proportion to your ability to establish rapport.

Finally, successful people fail. The critical difference between those who succeed and those who don't is in their mindset. Achievers make mistakes, but they do not allow mistakes to define who they are. They fail but they do not allow failure to set the terms for how they live. Instead, failure is an opportunity. Yes, I know this has become something of a cliché, but it's true. A setback gives you an opportunity to pause and assess your actions, to make adjustments, and to change direction if need be. On the other hand, a setback can give you a reason to quit. Successful people might consider quitting an option, but not for long. They keep pushing forward, battered and bruised, because they believe in themselves and in their goals.

Of the five qualities of success how many of them do you have right now? Can you identify what you need to improve on, learn about, or practice more in order to become first rate at what you do and to achieve level of professional fulfillment that you want?

Mapping with Your Mental GPS

There's an interesting skill associated with success that I've seen in some of the people I've coached. Successful people have an internal guidance system that gives them the ability to form a mental image that maps out the directions for any desired destination. It's the ability to construct a mental route to their goal. There may be changes along the way, of course, with ups and downs or an unexpected detour, but the goal stays always in sight, success inevitable. It's like having a self-generating GPS of Success.

This is not as crazy as it may sound. If I want to drive to a specific place that I have never been to before, I simply use the GPS in my car to calculate my route by entering the exact street address of where I want to go. In fact, I would enter the zip code, too. Once this information is plugged into the GPS and I've hit the enter button, all I need to do is follow the directions.

I don't ever argue with my GPS. (If you argue with yours, we have an entirely different conversation!) I take this right, that left, go west here, travel south there, and ta-da! I arrive at my destination!

Here is my question to you: Do you believe you can do the same thing with your life and your goals? If you don't know (or if you think I might be a little bit crazy just for asking), that's okay. I believe you do have a mental GPS system that is just waiting to be put to use. I've experienced it in my own life, and I have witnessed it in others. Your mind has the power to map a route to success and it's up to you to follow that route to your goal.

Whether the GPS of Success is a learned skill or a gift at birth (who knows?) all of us are genetically coded to go out in the world and get what we want (Chomsky, 2006). The quest to reach for what lies just ahead is a fundamental human condition that transcends the raw need to survive and gives meaning and purpose to our lives. These are advantages that should not be taken for granted.

Connect with your mental GPS. It is your inner guide to success and proof that the human mind is far more powerful than we can imagine.

Honestly! You have nothing to lose by trying this. Believe in the destination; believe in the power of YES, and you can accomplish amazing things.

The magic begins when you know your destination—your goal—and you believe in it. It becomes a part of your chemistry, your way of relating to the world. And so it is that every step closer to achieving your goal is another step closer to the habit of success! Your mind will know what to do without question; you will take the next step forward simply because it is necessary to the process. It's weird how it starts to happen automatically: when you believe in the destination, success will follow.

Still, I do not think that success comes along suddenly like an epiphany. Rarely does it explode on the scene in a once in a lifetime flash of brilliance. The truth is, there's no quick fix or easy way out of whatever it is you've been doing the same way for so long. Success is earned through the hard work of trial and error; it's tough, and to get it, you've got to be tougher. Heck, if it were easy, everyone would be doing it. They're not. What most of them are doing, in fact, is giving up on the very first fail. Wimps!

Well, there's no wimps here! The bottom line is this: being successful is perfectly legal. But so is selling yourself short. It's your decision. Which way do you want to go?

RESPONSIBILITY

What would you attempt to do if you knew you would not fail?
— *Robert Schuler*

Certain words represent key ideas for achieving success. (Hint: some are found in the chapter titles. Responsibility and Attitude, for example.) Each chapter will focus on one of these ideas, first by defining the word, and then by going deeper into how that concept can be used to learn a new habit and maximize your potential.

This chapter focuses on responsibility. The word responsibility has three definitions. One is to have a duty to deal with something or someone; the second means being held accountable or to blame for something; and the third definition is to have the authority (or ability) to act and make decisions without direct supervision (Agnes, 2010).

You may be wondering why I want to take the time to define words that you are already familiar with. Why? Because words are important. Whether spoken, written, or thought, words tell us what things are.

They describe our world while also having the power to shape it.

Socrates taught the ancient Greeks that wisdom begins with knowing the definition of terms. The definition effects how we think about the thing a word represents; how we think about a word will influence how we respond to it in a physical sense, therefore, if we change the way we think about a given word—for example, from the passive sense to the active—we should be able to change our behavior as it relates to that word.

Challenge One

Here's a simple challenge to demonstrate the power of words and how they interact with our habits. The next time someone asks "How are you?" respond with a confident, powerful voice, "I'm terrific!" You will probably feel a physical reaction. This is a signal that the word terrific has sent a message to your subconscious mind, and if you do this same thing repeatedly (that is, respond with the word terrific!) your subconscious mind will hear the message and start designing your reality to be consistent with your words and your conscious thoughts. I'll come back to this idea later on, but let's get back to the subject of responsibility.

30

Habit replacement therapy defines responsibility as taking ownership of your actions and thoughts throughout the day. It means taking ownership for the thoughts and attitudes that effect those actions and being aware of the fact that what you do and what you say can have an impact on others.

Make your thoughts positive. Wouldn't it be great if it were possible to go through life without making a single mistake? Mistakes and failures are a part of the human condition. Life can be a messy business. You will make mistakes and suffer through your share of failures, especially while you learn something new. Take an action-oriented attitude towards failure. Pay attention to the underlying message without beating yourself up with a barrage of self-defeating messages. Own it and move forward.

Actions + Thoughts + Future = Your Goals

Building a Powerful Morning Habit
If you are going to make the kind of changes that transform your life for the better, the best way to start is by making small changes in your day to day routine. Take an assessment of your

daily schedule or regular activities. Break it down. Your aim is to identify activities that serve no useful purpose or that set you back, and replace them with habits that are consistent with your goals. Do it now! Do not even think about putting this off until tomorrow. It's that important.

Think about your typical morning. Most of us have a set of routine behaviors that are so ingrained we don't even know what they are. Do you have a morning routine that boosts your energy and sharpens your thinking? Or do you go through the motions, bleary-eyed and foggy? Do you wake up excited about the opportunities in the day ahead? Or not? If you are among the bleary-eyed masses, then it's time to disrupt the routine!

I personally start every day the same way. As soon as I wake up, I do a 20 minute meditation. Don't make this complicated. Meditation just means to turn your thoughts inward. It may take some practice, especially if you're an uber-energy type A personality, but the great thing is that you will feel the benefits even if you devote as little as 3 to 5 minutes a day to quiet reflection. When I first started meditation I used a guided method. (This is a great way to go for hesitant first timers. I recommend Kelly

Howell's guided meditation.) Now I just create my own. Whether guided or solo, the basics are the same. Play meditation music (available free on YouTube) to help your concentration, and visualize your life exactly the way you want it to be.

If you have trouble forming a mental picture of your ideal life, there's a problem. Take the time to think about what you want in life. Break it down into specific terms. It's not enough, for instance, to know you want more happiness. Happiness is great, but take it further. What would make your life happier? Remember to be specific. Write it down, name names, or even draw a picture.

Then start thinking about what you need to do to make it possible. This is important. Take charge of creating the life you want to live. Later on we'll take a closer look at visualization and how it can help you achieve your goals. For now, the important thing is to make a decision as to how you want your life to look, then play this image in your mind while the meditation music plays in the background.

To review, start with the guided method if you're new to meditation. There's a wide choice of free programs available online. Choose a few titles that interest you and try them out until you find what works. It may be difficult to calm your mind in the beginning. This is normal. It might even seem like the harder you try to quiet your thoughts, the noisier your mind gets. Don't let this frustrate you. Give it some time. Practice every morning for at least a week or two and it will get easier. As it does, you will start to experience the benefits of meditation: less stress throughout the day, an increase in the ability to learn and concentrate, improved emotional regulation, and an overall feeling of well-being.

After a few minutes of meditation, I recommend that you do some form of physical activity. Yes, I'm talking about a daily morning work out. I'm kind of a nut about this but you don't have to be. Regardless of your physical condition, there is a suitable workout for you. Be sure to check with your doctor who can provide suggestions for your specific needs. You don't need to start training for a marathon, just establish a morning physical routine that gets the blood flowing and the metabolism cranking. You will be amazed by the positive effect this morning workout will have on everything else you do throughout the day. It's kind of like money. It doesn't make anything worse!

After the workout I find something on YouTube to watch and listen to while I'm getting ready and having breakfast. There is a wealth of great stuff on YouTube, and it's all free. Wayne Dyer, Tony Robbins, Deepak Chopra, the list goes on and on. I'm guessing that right now you probably have the TV on anyway, maybe half-listening to the news. I'm also guessing that there is very little going on in the news that is positive right now—or ever, as far as I can tell. Stop listening to that negative stuff right now! It does nothing to improve your mindset. Instead, watch positive videos you can easily find on YouTube and see what happens in just 30 days.

Now on to what can be a very sensitive subject for many of us. Food. How well are you eating? It definitely matters. Digestion is the single most energy-intensive process your body does. (Think Thanksgiving dinner!) So be kind to yourself by choosing to eat small healthy meals that provide most of your energy for the day so you can get to all the things you want to accomplish. I routinely eat six small meals a day that add up to roughly 2500 calories. I have found through many years of experimenting that this is what works for me. It may be different for you. Pay attention to your body. It will help you out if you are listening and if you are being honest with yourself.

I know, I know. It probably sounds like I'm telling you that all of this is easy, that you only have to change this one thing—sure, one thing that happens be everything! It might very well be everything, but it sure doesn't have to happen overnight. Heck, it can't happen overnight. I'll be the first to admit that some of these changes are pretty hard to do. It is. But the payoff is huge. So start slow. Keep it simple. And don't allow discouragement or frustration to get in your way. This is your life!

I remember 6 years ago when I wanted to get into the shape I'm currently in. I figured out that it would take me anywhere from 12 to 18 months. Guess what. It actually took more than 3 years. Did I feel discouraged on some days? You bet I did. Here's a thought. It takes work to make changes, to get up earlier, to workout every morning, to act and think in a positive way. Yet it also takes work to stay put where you currently are or even to go downhill, especially when you beat yourself up for it day after day after day. Get the point? You are going to do one of those three things anyway, so why not make a commitment now to begin the right work. Quit selling yourself short. There have been plenty of short sales in the housing market these past several years. Don't allow yourself to become one of them. It's time to write a new story, and once again for those of you who might have forgotten, take it one day at a time!

It takes daily effort to replace the old way of thinking with a new way of thinking. I've been there and I know there are rough days when the world appears to be pushing against you. On days like this when things get tough, your inner chatter can turn ugly and fearful. Fear is a devastating force that works against your efforts to build a new life. It can lead you to question yourself. "What if I get there and I don't like it? What if I fail all together? What if I need help? What will I do then?"

These are all natural concerns, but if left unchecked, they can keep you from making sound decisions and moving forward. There is only one thing more powerful than fear and that's the belief in one's self. The more you fill your head with belief in yourself, the less room there will be for fear. It just takes time, and time is one thing we all have in equal measure.

Challenge Two

Here's a goal that I want you to start working on right away. Empty your mind of the old thinking and replace it with new thinking. Be patient. Remember that once you master faith in yourself, you will automatically conquer fear. (By the way, throughout the book you'll find specific activities and tips designed to strengthen your confidence and knock out fear.)

From now on, your challenge is to think about fear in a new way. Fear is just an old habit that stands between you and your goals. Replace the old habit of fear with the new habit of belief in yourself.

Stop Holding Yourself Back!

You are where you are today because of what you've been thinking and doing for a long time. If you are not satisfied with where you are, change it. People do have the ability to change. Remember, we are incredibly good at it, so good in fact that our ability to change and adapt has been a driving force in our success as a species (Diamond, 2006). It does take some courage and a measure of risk, but when you recognize this and start taking steps towards a new way of thinking and a new way of acting, your goals will be easier to achieve. Don't forget, it took time to get to where you are today. It's going to take time to make changes.

Overcoming a bad habit is really all about a single 24 hour period. Take it one day at a time. This is your responsibility, your daily target, to maximize one 24 hour period at a time. When you've made it through the first 30 day cycle, you will see some noticeable changes. After 90 days it gets even easier and those changes really start to pay off.

Directing your energy at incremental steps (such as taking things one day at a time), will help you stay focused on the daily process instead of worrying about the final result. Success is the natural outcome as each day's progress builds on the day before, every action building on the previous action. The first habit you work on is the most difficult one to achieve, the second habit a little easier than the first, and so on.

Your ego will tell you that all this new activity is going to hurt. It's going to hurt for a long time. Your ego is like that pushy telemarketer who won't stop trying to convince you that you don't need to change. "You're fine just the way you are!" Understand that this is the ego's job. Ignore it.

Look, you would not be reading this book if you didn't want to make at least some changes. Accept the fact that it's going to take some work and it's going to be a challenge. There will come a time or two when you'll want to quit altogether. Sure, it would be easier to keep on doing the same things every day in the same way you've been doing them. But the reward, and ultimately your life, are worth taking responsibility and doing what it takes to change.

It's your choice whether to stay the same or to make progress. I guarantee that when you make the commitment to a new life, a new way of thinking, a new plan for daily action, by the end of the day—even if you feel more exhausted than you have ever felt in your life—you will never have felt better.

Inside the acorn lives the potential for the mighty oak.

Are Your Thoughts Working For or Against You?

If you were to continue with your current self-talk, would you be able to achieve your goals? Responsibility means you are in charge of your thoughts just as you are in charge of your actions. You control whether your thoughts and actions result in a daily sentence of punishment, or instead having them be like a gift you give to yourself.

Here's another way of looking at it. Would you talk to your spouse, your kids, or your friends ... the same way you talk to yourself? For most of you, I hope not. If you did, you might just find yourself in the middle of a divorce, disowned by your kids, and all your friends jumping overboard. Ouch! So much for punishment.

Self-talk that has the effect of a gift would sound something like this: "I am the most powerful person I have ever met." Stop. Do that repeatedly over time—make it your mental mantra—and soon you will program yourself to be that person. This is one of the greatest gifts you can give yourself. (And no, this has nothing to do with being overly self-centered. This is empowerment.)

Again, I'm not saying this is easy. Sometimes we have to fight the past to get to a better tomorrow. If you dwell on it, the past can turn into a Ninja assassin waiting to strike down your every forward move. Each of us has a past to contend with. The past is what got us here, after all. Every saint has a past, every sinner a future.

Acknowledge your own past, pay it a ceremonial bow, and let it go.

Okay, I may be kidding a little to make a point. It's all right to laugh and have some fun with it. The takeaway is that this is your life and you have the power to make it the way you want it. From this moment on, will your days be a sentence or a gift? One or the other, the choice is yours and the outcome is your responsibility. What will it be?

COMMITMENT

Commitment is an act, not a word.
—John Paul-Sartre

Most of us think of a commitment as being dedicated to a cause or activity (like a commitment to excellence), or to an engagement or obligation that (usually) restricts our freedom of action (like a business commitment). There's more, however, to making—and keeping—a commitment than the standard definition might suggest, especially when building the habits of success. For example, a commitment demands the active engagement of your mind. Engagement in this sense means to establish and maintain the daily mindset that supports the path to your goals.

A commitment is a promise; it's giving your word that you will follow through to the best of your ability and take responsibility for the outcome, even if you fail. Every commitment counts. Each one is important, especially when it involves other people. Your word should mean something even when the promise you make is only to yourself. A commitment alone does not guarantee success. If you fail but keep working at it, your actions will honor your commitment and success will follow.

Motivation

Whether you commit to a new goal or to an entirely new way of life, don't be surprised if the first two or three weeks are easy, followed by a frustrating uphill climb. The culprit is most often a loss of motivation. Let's say your goal is to lose weight and gain better health. You make a commitment to a new diet that is designed to accomplish your goal. You plan for success and enthusiastically print out the do's and don'ts of your new diet, pinning them up strategically around the house—on the refrigerator door, inside the pantry, up on the bathroom mirror, as a lining for the top drawer of your desk. All of your friends are aware of the impending change and are behind you all the way. You've managed to recruit some of them to join you so you won't have to diet alone. You have taken measures to remove temptation by throwing out every offending morsel of junk food, and written up a weekly shopping list that follows the diet plan posted on the fridge. Success? You are prepared!

During this planning and implementation period your motivation is strong enough that even if you falter at first, you will quickly bounce back on track. A few weeks go by and then what? Your motivation drops a bit. Your self-talk chatters on unchecked until you have convinced yourself that a break is what you need and it won't make a difference if you go off your diet for a day. Let's make that two days. Oh, what the heck, you can start over next week. Keep this up though, and your inner voice can turn against you. Who needs to lose a few pounds anyway?

Momentum

Well, it does not have to be that way. You can overcome a loss of motivation or a wobbly commitment by taking action. Knowing that boredom and complacency are common elements that chip away at your momentum, you can prepare a contingency plan to get through the down days with your goals and your pride intact. What follows is a short list of practical tips to help you emerge triumphant from a slump.

1. Goals should be realistic and meaningful. Know clearly the reasons for each goal. Avoid

having unclear goals and unclear reasons because they lead to poor results.

2. Set up a dream board. Cut out magazine pictures to illustrate your goals and pin them on a bulletin board where you will see them every day. The house of your dreams, the car you've wanted since you were twelve, or that great vacation spot to take the whole family … if you want it and there's a picture of it, pin it on your dream board as a daily reminder.

3. Create a personal mantra or daily affirmations for the things you want to accomplish. For example: if I weigh 200 pounds and I want to weigh 175, I'll tell myself, "I weigh 175 pounds!" Here's another example: I want to make $200,000 a year. My daily affirmation is "I make $200,000 a year." You could also write a formal mission statement that serves as an organizing principle for a major goal or even for your life.

4. Draw a map or write up an action plan for your goals. This becomes the contract that formalizes your commitment to change. It doesn't have to be complicated, just specific, appropriate to the goal, and actionable.

5.   Switch on your "autopilot" to get through those days when you don't feel like following the plan. Easier said than done, I know. Do it anyway. It takes a strong level of commitment to summon the self-discipline to stick to the plan when you're tired or feeling discouraged about your progress. Winners do it even when they don't feel like it. That's why they win. You can do it too. The feeling of not wanting to do new activities will go away quickly as long as you do them even on the days when you don't want to, just for a little while.

Know Your Commitments

Do you know what your commitments are? Look beyond the obvious (family, friends, health and well-being), and take into account your values and your behavior. Are you more focused on certain things, do you believe in certain values, or do you act towards someone in a way that defines their importance to you? But does the fact that something or someone is important to you also mean that you are committed to them?

There are different levels of commitment, of course. This is evident when you notice yourself being more focused and involved with some activities over others. Does this mean that you can be a little committed to one thing and more committed to another? Is the current state of your life what you are committed to? Or have you ceased to take action because of the struggles you know you might have to face?

We have all been through the process of setting goals and resolutions with full intent of following through, and we have all slipped back into old habits, giving in or giving up altogether. Every one of us has been haunted by the excuses and the "yeah, buts" that have cost who knows how many lost opportunities for personal growth and improvement. If we truly want to grow as individuals we have to find that area in our lives where commitment supersedes comfort. Do your commitments live up to your dreams? What is the one thing you would choose to do even in the absence of external reward and feedback?

Commitment is what drives us to take action. It is that which we would be willing to give 100 percent to achieve while putting aside personal gain and recognition. Committed is the willingness to do whatever it takes to fulfill and follow through on a responsibility. It may not even be what we most enjoy, but our commitment means we are going to do it regardless.

Commitment is essential to the process of achieving your highest goals. Being dedicated is a part of personal growth and rising to the next level.

Each of us comes from a unique environment and are dedicated to different values and countless missions. Regardless of these differences and our chosen direction in life, there are three shared elements that keep us committed to our goals: sacrifice, purpose, and determination.

Sacrifice
A fundamental means of knowing we are committed is when we are willing to make a sacrifice in order to achieve our goals. Consider the young athlete willing to practice for hours every day, or those in the military who are willing to make the ultimate sacrifice of their lives in the name of their country. Commitment through sacrifice conveys a willingness to stand by our commitment even if it means giving up comforts or accepting disruptions in other areas of our lives.

Purpose
Commitment requires us to find meaning and purpose behind the mission we are pursuing.

Having a meaningful purpose that moves us to act is half the battle of achieving our goals. A meaningful purpose is the engine that drives us forward. It's what gets us out of bed each day and keeps us awake with excitement at night. In the absence of purpose, the ability to sustain a commitment becomes difficult if not impossible. Successful commitments are connected to that which ignites our passion for life.

Determination

Determination and commitment go hand in hand. There will be inevitable setbacks along the way to achieving success, and without the determination to overcome these setbacks, commitment begins to waver. We must face obstacles with resiliency and a willingness to take the necessary steps to overcome barriers. Instead of viewing an unexpected outcome as a problem, we can view it as a challenge. Determination allows us to perceive these challenges as part of the larger process of accomplishment that we are committed to.

Knowing the areas of commitment in your life can greatly simplify and sharpen your focus.

Take it further by formulating a plan of action that will keep you moving towards your goals, goals that provide meaningful purpose and fulfillment.

CONSISTENCY

Today was good. Today was fun. Tomorrow is another one.
−Dr. Seuss

If you want to maximize your results, make your daily actions consistent with your goals. This might seem obvious, but I am still astonished by the number of people who will plan their goals with tremendous energy and enthusiasm, and then go about their daily lives doing everything but goal-oriented activities. A few weeks down the road, these same people wonder why they haven't made better progress towards their goals!

Consistency is the steady level of achievement or effect over a period of time, or being in a state of compatibility or agreement with something. Remember that habit replacement therapy emphasizes action and process. From now on be aware of your actions and whether or not they support your goals and your mission in life. The more your thoughts and behavior are in tune with the things you want to accomplish, the more progress you will make towards the results you desire.

There's an additional positive side effect that comes from having your daily actions consistent with your goals. You'll feel great about yourself. This alone will have a significant impact on your life because when you feel good about yourself—especially while you are actively learning or improving a skill or habit—your confidence and momentum gets an extra boost. It's like money in the bank for your energy level. Your brain picks up that feel good message and responds by creating a framework of neural connections that support all those great success messages. Over time, you will have a positive feedback loop that will refine your focus and drive you forward towards your goals. As you experience more progress and more success, you'll continue to feel great and will be better able to maintain momentum, and this positive cycle keeps repeating itself. Wow. You're getting pretty good at this!

Athletes have long known about the big payoff that comes when their daily actions are consistent with their goals. The most successful athletes have developed strategies that either maximize the advantages of their strengths, or take what others have judged to be a disadvantage and turned it on its head. Either way, the result is a win. The real stories of two well-known athletes are great examples of these strategies in action.

Bumble Bees and Flipper Feet

Michael Phelps

Olympic Gold-medalist and record-smashing swimmer Michael Phelps is a veteran athlete at the ripe old age of 28. Phelps has won more medals—an incredible 22 wins out of 24 races—than any other Olympic competitor … in *any* sport. Phelps has maximized his natural strengths and follows a rigorous practice schedule when training for a race. His arm span is that of a person 3 inches taller, his knees are double-jointed, and (this next one is impressive), he can rotate his size 14 feet a full 15 degrees more than the average person, a physical feature that Phelps has learned to use like he would a pair of scuba flippers, pushing off the wall to cover nearly half the length of the pool using only his feet.

Tom Brady

When the New England Patriots drafted Tom Brady more than a decade ago, it caused a stir in the NFL. Here was this round six player whose statistics had some people wondering how the Patriots could show such an apparent lapse in judgment. Tom Brady does not look like a winner on paper. Neither do bumble bees.

It's true. Bumblebees look bad on paper from a statistical perspective. They ought to be gathering nectar on foot, but there they are, buzzing around the garden like a slap in the face of nature. It's astonishing, really. Now, I'm not going to try to convince you that Brady can fly, of course, but the math tells us he is a terrible football player. Get him on the playing field though, and he is off the hook! Why? One answer is that those bad stats are a one-dimensional measurement. But this is only half of the story. Brady knows the numbers but he sees beyond them, pointing out that stats are no substitute for commitment or competitiveness, two unbeatable qualities that put him far ahead of the game.

Brady and Phelps are highly successful in their careers. Brady's ability to transcend the disadvantages shown in his paper stats, and Phelps' ability to take advantage of his unique physical characteristics demonstrate two different strategies for success in action. Both strategies can be applied outside of sports. And anyone can build their own positive feedback loop to achieve success for any goal, in any field.

So far, we have been focused on positive habits and measuring success. Have you ever thought about measuring life? In fact, the areas of life that have the greatest importance are un-measurable! If you were able to weigh a person who has just died, 5 minutes before and again at 5 minutes after death, the two weights would be pretty much the same. What, then, does life weigh? We can agree for the sake of argument that life is the force (or the energy), that keeps your heart beating and this, in turn, is the source of energy that flows through your body and keeps you alive.

But what exactly is that force? Who knows. It's one of life's mysteries that can only mean one thing: each of us has exactly the same amount as everyone else. You are either alive, or not. It does not matter where you are, where you've been, or even how you got here. As long as you have a pulse, you have the ability to create major changes in your life. Human beings are masters of change and adaptability. Our rise to the top of the Earth's food chain and our survivability that has far exceeded all other species that have ever lived on this planet—ever—is proof that even you can change. Congratulations!

Look, if you had one shot, one opportunity to seize everything you ever wanted; One moment. Would you capture it, or just let it slip through your fingers?
—Eminem

I love those words and here's why. You will have several opportunities to do something you have always wanted to do. You can fail. And fail, and fail again. But as long as you keep getting up and trying, that moment of opportunity will come again! Break off the rear view mirrors of your life. You've spent more than enough time on the "what if's" and the "if only I had's." Stop it! Don't look back. Look forward. The only requirement for membership in the goal achievers club is to have a pulse and the right ATTITUDE.

Maxwell's Art of Failing Forward

John Maxwell, in his book *Attitude 101*, describes a mindset he calls failing forward." Every year, a ceramics teacher begins the semester by dividing her class into two random groups. Students sitting on the left side of the classroom are told they will be graded according to the amount of work they produced, while the students sitting on the right side are told their grades will be based on the quality of their work.

How could she determine the student's grades in an equitable manner? She used a surprisingly simple method. For the students on the left, she brought in a scale and weighed each student's work. An A grade was given for 50 pounds of work, a B for 40 pounds, a C for 30 pounds. The students who where graded on quality however, had one project assigned: to make a single ceramic pot as perfectly as possible to receive an A. When the semester ended and it was time to grade the students, the results were not what she expected.

The group who produced the highest quality work turned out to be the same group who were graded only on quantity. These were the students on the left. But why? Because, while the quality group sat around theorizing about how to produce perfection in order to get an A and with little to show for it at semester's end, the quantity group was busy making pots, one after another after another, and each time they churned out a pot, they learned from their mistakes, and they kept getting better and faster at making pots.

It doesn't make any difference whether you are in school, at work, playing a sport, or in a relationship. One of the most important things you can do to reach your goals and achieve your dreams, is to consistently practice the necessary skills every day. And don't be afraid to fail early and often. The best time to make mistakes is when you first start learning something new. This is a great time to practice being fearless with failure. Sara Blakely, one of the first female self-made billionaires and the creator of Spanks (a brand of women's shapewear), has said that growing up, her father would encourage her to fail, asking her to tell him what she had failed at that week. This may seem like an odd thing for a parent to ask, but Blakely explains that her father's intent was not to emphasize failure. It was really all about the failure to try.

Focus

Where focus goes, energy flows.
— *Tony Robbins*

This chapter is about focus and confidence. Confidence is having the feeling or belief that you (or someone else) can do something well or succeed at a goal. Confidence also refers to a feeling of certainty in a particular event or outcome, or that an idea or statement is true. If your confidence is low, it's fairly easy to figure out what can happen to your goals. On the one hand, you'll question whether you have the ability to be successful, and on the other, you won't believe in your own goals—and that's about the worst place you can be in terms of success. It's important to strengthen your confidence while you work on building a new habit because it's the most effective tool you can have to fight the fear of falling on your face.

If your confidence is low, there are specific actions you can take to turn things around. Start by feeding your mind a constant stream of affirmative thoughts. This does take some practice but the payoff is well worth the effort.

The goal is to keep your self-talk focused with positive statements that encourage you to believe you can, and will, achieve the desired result.

Once your confidence is secure, it will be easier to ignore distractions and stay on track throughout the day. When your focus is clear, you'll waste less time and have more energy for the things that really matter.

What if you have trouble concentrating on what you need to accomplish? The ability to remain focused on one thing for the time it takes to see it all the way through to completion is vital to success. Without this persistence, it will take a lot longer to reach your goals, leading to an increase in the likelihood that you'll abandon them all together.

People fight taking things one day at a time, confident and focused. Instead, they always want the day to hurry up. We don't want to age, yet we rush through life to get to the finish line. On Mondays, we wish it was a Wednesday; on Wednesday, we're longing for a Friday, and every day, we watch the clock and ask ourselves "Is it 5:00 yet?" If this sounds like you, it may be time to rethink your career choice. People! Stop looking at the clock—it's time to get real!

Most people exist from one paycheck to another, never realizing their full potential to create the life they want for themselves. Look, your life is your responsibility. Get up and do something. Now. Not later. Get your confidence on and get some progress done. Make a decision. Set a simple goal. Take one day and do one thing. And make it spectacular! One day at a time, follow the plan, stick to the schedule, eliminate distractions, keep your hands to yourself, and don't hurt anybody. If you fail, get up like you meant it and try again. See? You can do it.

I love using AA as an example because I have personal experience with it. It works. I know this because it saved my life. AA has a book out called *The 12 Steps for Everyone*. Get a copy and read it. Or if you think you might have a problem with drugs or alcohol, read AA's big book. Better still, read it even if you don't have a problem. It's a great book.

One reason why AA's 12-step program has shown a history of success is because the program asks you to be brutally honest with yourself. For the alcoholic, there's also the addition of new behavior that flies in the face of an alcoholic's daily drinking routine. It's a tough change to stop drinking and start hanging around a group of sober people. Yuk.

For the alcoholic, this reality at first has them thinking, "poor me (when it used to be pour me a drink), this is my life. This is no life that I want." Unfortunately, every alcoholic has to hit bottom before they can look up. AA calls this the gift of desperation. (You may be able to see how similar this is to failure.) But if they keep going they soon begin to realize they have been given a gift for life that may not come again.

Another important aspect of AA is in order for it to work, you must stick with the program long enough for the miracle to happen. It's the same with any change in behavior or habit, just as it is when you are taking on a challenge as big as creating a whole new life for yourself. Some days are more difficult than others; some days you just have to take the body through the motions while you wait for the mind to catch up. (And it will if you keep working through the correct motions.)

One more thought about hitting bottom, what AA refers to as the gift of desperation. Just as it is with any failure, you can choose to turn this into the best thing that has ever happened to you. It is a choice.

You need leverage to make major changes. Take a look at your past. Now, don't stare! Just take a quick look. Obviously, you are reading this book for a reason. You really need to be fed up with the way things have been and you really need to be ready to make some changes. You can choose to view this moment of self-awareness as a gift and use it as the leverage you need to create the new life you are looking for.

Many people I know are fed up with too many problems. You didn't come in to this world equipped with a standard set of problems. You have practiced, drilled, rehearsed, and created every single problem you currently have. Fun to think about, right? It's time to take out the trash. Consider this: you don't carry your household garbage with you everywhere you go, do you? (Please don't tell me your answer is yes.) Imagine, you. A giant Hefty bag slung over your shoulder, stomping around the neighborhood like the Santa of trash while screaming wide-eyed tots take off running every time you appear. You may be laughing but it's only because I've painted a picture for you. What I'm really talking about is the trash in your mind. Just because you can't see something, doesn't mean it isn't effecting you. Throw out the garbage and get to work, one day at a time, confident and focused.

Reality Distortion Fields

If this is the first time you have seen the words "Reality Distortion Fields" (RDF) you might think it's the title of a Star Trek episode or maybe a sexy new cocktail. The term actually did come from a Star Trek episode, but the idea gained a footing in the business world when it was used to describe the leadership style of Apple computer's founder, Steve Jobs. Jobs was known for attaining the seemingly impossible by persuading his employees and creative teams to alter their view of reality (that is, to suspend their belief) so they were certain they possessed the ability to accomplish extraordinarily difficult—if not unreasonable—goals.

The elements that make up a reality distortion field start with an unrelenting commitment to a goal and a "no fail" attitude towards finding the perfect solution to a problem. Using the skill of persuasion, an RDF inspires others to ignore the cold hard facts of reality and to believe in the impossible, at least for as long as it takes to reach the goal. Thus, employees who found themselves caught in Jobs' reality distortion field were convinced that they could fix any problem put to them.

Business leaders have used RDF techniques to motivate their employees so they will meet demanding company goals, and because it is such an effective method of persuasion, it is a natural fit for sales. My interest, however, is in finding out new ways to us it as a tool for individuals to convince themselves of their ability to re-shape reality in such a way that the world works with rather than against them. With the ability to simplify problems and temporarily suspend reality, RDF may help us see beyond a muddle and move forward without getting stuck. In other words, RDF encourages imaginative problem-solving and a mindset that believes the solutions are easily within reach. You might have experienced something like this during your daily visualization or meditation. Let's switch things up by adding RDF to your next goal. Your mindset could make you unstoppable!

Think about it. What if you were as serious about convincing yourself into success as Jobs was in taking on the task of convincing his people that they could produce whatever he was pitching? Even if your level of commitment doesn't match the fanaticism Jobs was known to have, I promise it will help considerably in the quest to achieve your goals.

Creative Visualization

If you're one of the estimated 35 million people who has spent an evening or two watching reruns of Star Trek, you might remember the holodeck, a virtual reality playroom where the crew could become the actors in their own imaginary worlds brought to life. They could practice daring combat maneuvers with a hostile cyborg or play a winning game of chess against an imaginary grand master. Anything a crewmember could think of, the holodeck could create in a three dimensional virtual world.

For most of us, virtual reality is still largely a thing reserved for high tech, space-age applications. But did you know that your brain is able to function like a virtual reality generator, and that you can take advantage of this as a shortcut to your goals. The ability to generate reality is but one of the incredible things we have only begun to learn about our amazing human brains. Captain Kirk may have claimed that space was the final frontier, but back here on Earth, the final frontier is all in our heads.

Remember when I asked you to change the way you responded to the question, "How are you?" This was intended to show your fabulous brain in action as it constructed a new virtual reality out of the message it received (feeling good), that was in turn reinforced by an increase in physical energy and a positive attitude.

Creative visualization refers to the practice of seeking to effect the outer world by changing one's inner thoughts and expectations. It arose in the United States during the nineteenth century using techniques proposed by Wallace Wattles in *The Science of Getting Rich*. Wattles proposed the idea that creative visualization was the key to realizing one's goals, a practice that has its origins in the Hindu faith.

Actor Jim Carrey once told a story about his life that illustrates how creative visualization can be a powerful a tool for change. Carrey wrote a 10 million dollar check to himself in 1987, when he was still struggling as a comedian. He dated the check for "Thanksgiving 1995" and added the notation, "for acting services rendered." For the next 8 years, he imagined himself cashing this 10 million dollar check, until one day in 1994 when he was paid 10 million dollars for his role in the hit movie *Dumb and Dumber*. It may have taken 8 years, but wow, what a payoff!

Creative visualization was regarded as "new age hype" for many years, but research has shown repeatedly that there is a strong scientific basis for how and why visualization works. Today, the benefits gained by creative visualization are well understood. When we visualize ourselves performing an action, we stimulate the same regions in the brain that are stimulated when we physically perform that same action.

For example, when you visualize lifting your right hand to scratch your nose, the mental picture stimulates the same neural locations in the brain that are activated when you physically lift your right hand up to scratch your nose. Our brains appear to make no distinction between the image of the action and the action itself; new pathways and neural connections are created (i.e., our brain's virtual reality), regardless of the source of the message. And it's the message that holds the key for habit replacement therapy. This shared area of the brain that activates when we imagine an action and perform it has been supported throughout the scientific literature on the subject.

There are numerous examples of the way visualization increases brain activity in victims of stroke. When a person has a stroke due to a blood clot in a brain artery, blood cannot reach the tissue that the artery once fed with oxygen and nutrients. That brain tissue dies. This tissue death spreads to the surrounding area that does not receive the blood any more. However, if a person with this kind of localized stroke is able to form a mental image of moving the affected arm or leg, blood flow within the brain at the affected site increases and the surrounding brain tissue may be saved. Imagining moving a limb, even after it has been paralyzed after a stroke, increases brain blood flow enough to diminish the amount of tissue death. This is powerful support of the effectiveness of creative visualization.

Using Imagery to Maximize Your Potential
Tell your brain about your plan to maximize your potential using one thousand words and your brain is likely to get bored mid-way and take a nap. But draw it a colorful picture of your plan and the response is rapturous attention. Your brain has no trouble with the words but who doesn't love a great illustration? Can we apply this in a way that maximizes our own brain's potential?

Try one or all four of the following tips:

1. If you have no idea how to act, start by imagining what you want. What you want will not come immediately, but imagining is a way of getting the process started quickly. For example, if you want to start a home-based baking business, start by imagining being in the kitchen surrounded by cakes and cookies that you are taking out of the oven. Draw a sketch of this, and then draw sketches that come before and after this. The more clearly and repetitively you outline this, the more likely it will be that you will succeed.

2. If you have had a setback, do not give up. Keep the blood flowing to the area of the brain that will execute your action plan by focusing on what you want. People are often distracted by their fears. All this will do is increase blood flow to the regions in your brain that will stop your actions. Remember, a failure is not a final statement that you will not succeed. It is information that your vision has to be changed, refined, or simply repeated.

3. When you start your visualization, construct the image when your mind is free of worries

and stress, even if you have to carve out an imaginary world to do this. When you visualize while worrying, it is like painting with a shaky brush. Calmness and peace increases the creativity of your mental brushstrokes.

4. If your confidence is low, use visualization of your goals to help increase your confidence. Practice makes perfect. Repeat these visualizations every day. As you imagine your goal and the process more clearly, your confidence will increase enough to execute on your desired goal.

These are just a few of the ways that visualization can help maximize your brain's awesome potential. Creative visualization is not the grown-up version of a child's game of make believe. It is one of many tools with principles grounded in science that can help you reach your goals. Practice using your mind to paint the pictures that you desire. When you do this, your brain will act in accordance with your vision. Just be aware of what you feed in to your brain: today's input will become tomorrow's reality.

PROCESS

The process guarantees the outcome.
−*Deepak Chopra*

Habit replacement is a process. Process is defined by Webster's as a series of actions or steps that are taken in order to achieve a particular end (Agnes, 2010). In habit replacement therapy, process is an ongoing series of actions that are performed on a daily basis in order to achieve a desired change. It's important that you practice the new behavior every day for at least a month in order to train both your mind and body to perform with little or no effort. (In other words, make it a habit to practice every day!)

The Courage to Win
Hundreds of athletes are gathered near the shore of Lake Mead in the early morning heat of the Nevada desert, temperatures already climbing towards 100 degrees. The crowd is growing anxious for the starting gun to signal the first Ironman 70.3 Silverman, a three-part

triathlon that demands the best of every athlete having the courage to compete.

The Silverman is 70.3 miles of kick ass in a single day: a 1.2 mile swim across Lake Mead, followed by a 56 mile bicycle tour across the hilly terrain of Lake Mead Mountain Reserve, ending with a 13.1 mile run through the neighborhoods of Henderson, Nevada.

I was there in support of my good friend Maverick who, by the end of the day, would add the Silverman to his hard-earned record of wins. My initial task was to paddle nearby in a kayak during the first leg of the race so I could shout out directions to help keep him swimming on course.

During the bicycle and running segments, my aim was to keep pace with Maverick, whose experience with endurance events was clearly evident, especially as we crossed the finish line. Maverick is proof in action that nothing can keep you from accomplishing your goals if you want them badly enough. What makes him such an outstanding role model and an inspiration to others? It would be enough to say that he has broken a few records over the years considering where he was back in 1997 when he first made the decision to tackle this demanding sport. He wasn't much of a swimmer, and his athletic experience was primarily in high school football, not exactly a sport well known for churning out long-distance runners.

If you didn't know him, you might think he had gone off the deep end for setting such a difficult goal, but Maverick's determination was immoveable. He was going to win this thing big, never mind that earlier this same year his doctor had declared him legally blind from a degenerative eye disease that was now threatening to limit his freedom.

The quest to compete in an Ironman became a centering force that fueled his commitment and kept him moving forward through progressively more difficult events and many long hours of practice. He went through more than one coach, numerous injuries, and with such poor eyesight, the number of bicycle crashes he suffered soon had his friends calling him Mav Crash Malech.

Swimming presented another big hurdle that once had him covering closer to 2 miles in a 1.2 mile swim as he zigzagged across a lake to reach the other side. In spite of the odds, he refused to give up, his perseverance finally paying off in 2004 when he became the first legally blind athlete to complete not one, but two Ironman World Championships.

Maverick is nothing short of courageous in his refusal to accept defeat. He would most likely tell you that he hopes his experience will inspire you to overcome whatever limitations you let stand in the way of your dreams. These limitations are no match for the power of you.

How Long Does It Take? Really.

I am often asked if a month is all it takes to create a new habit. The answer is that there is no single way to answer that question, at least not with a definitive yes or no. It can take as little as 30 days, or it can take a year or more, or anything in between because different people learn different things at different rates. What I can tell you is that 28 to 30 days is the average *minimum* time frame you can expect for a simple behavior change to take hold, although you should plan on it taking longer. Hey, don't forget though, the more you practice the easier it gets.

The process is crucial for your long term success. Those old routines that are now deeply rooted in your psyche because you have been doing them for so long, can also be maddeningly stubborn to quit. The longer a habit has been around and the more elaborate it is, the more resistant that habit is going to be when you set out to change it. Waking up at 6 AM instead of 8, for example, is relatively easy to work through compared to the whole trigger, ritual, reward cycle of a full blown addiction, an extreme form of habit that needs a great deal more time and focus. But that's okay. We expect this and plan appropriately.

When you know your goal is a demanding one and likely to require significant vigilance, give yourself extra planning time. Set a date far enough in advance so you can adequately prepare yourself. Be sure you set your schedule to regularly get enough sleep. Pay attention to what you eat so your energy level is high. Practice visualizing yourself going through the physical steps that will lead to success. If your old habit involves a particular time of day or a specific place that acts as a trigger point, imagine yourself doing the new action you plan to do in response to that trigger that will neutralize its power over you. Another strategy is to see if you can tie in your new habit with a routine that you already have so that the existing habit becomes a positive trigger for the new one.

Strengthen your resolve and practice the replacement behavior on a daily basis. Claim responsibility for your thoughts, words, and actions. Use affirmative statements and positive self-talk to shore up your mental courage and tenacity, and remind yourself that the bigger the challenge, the greater the reward!

Got it? Because there will be a quiz later on. I'm joking about the quiz of course, but there is a lot of information to remember. I warned you that change would be difficult but not impossible. For every kind of bad habit there's an expert or a program ready to guide you through the process to victory. Many of these programs focus on strategies, technologies, and training. But often that's not enough. When it comes to modifying deeply ingrained behavior, 12-step programs have a known track record through the combined use of incentives, celebration, peer pressure, coaching, negative reinforcement, and role models—a formula that has been successful in treating all sorts of troublesome behavior. If you need outside help to overcome a habit, a 12-step program is a good place to start.

Most of us try to tackle our bad habits on our own. It seems like the best way to reach a desired result would be to focus on that result, take action to move toward it, and judge each attempt by how closely you approximate it. But actually that approach is far from ideal. If you focus your attention and effort less on the results you're hoping for and more on the processes and techniques you use to get there, you will learn faster, become more successful, and ultimately be happier with the outcome.

By default human beings tend to be forward-looking, goal-pursuing, and results-oriented. Why? Because our evolutionary history has us wired for discontentment with the present. It is in our nature to strive for a better future. We are results-oriented because results are often easier to measure and evaluate than processes and because we know that others will judge us by our results. Unfortunately, this leads us to care too much what others think.

The better strategy is to focus on the process rather than the outcome. There are for several reasons why this is so. First, it gets rid of the static noise of external factors that only serve to distract you from your purpose. Another reason follows from the fact that success can be the result of a flawed effort and failure can be the result of a flawless effort. In those cases, judging performance by the outcome will reinforce the wrong techniques. You'll achieve mastery of a new skill more quickly if you can learn to detect those cases and reinforce the correct processes, whether or not they led to the desired outcome.

Also, a strategy that centers on process will encourage experimentation. If your focus is entirely on a specific desired result, you are far less willing to try a long shot, less inclined to experiment, less open to the joy of being spontaneous, and less likely to stumble on an even better outcome than the one you were aiming for.

Enjoy the process more. Regardless of our history, life is lived in the present, not the future. Happiness is a process, not a place. When your focus is on the process you engage more deeply with the present, allowing you to experience life more fully.

The process puts you in control. You have only partial control over whether you reach a specific external goal, but you have complete control over the process you use. Whether you give it your best effort is entirely within your power. Having an internal center of control leads to empowerment, higher self-esteem, and a more fulfilling level of success, all of which contribute in a meaningful sense to your overall life satisfaction.

Focusing on the process allows you to enjoy and benefit more from whatever the outcome is. In general, things rarely turn out exactly the way we expect them to. If your happiness is dependent on your success, and if you judge success based solely on a single outcome, you are more likely to experience greater levels of frustration and disappointment. Instead, if you can let go of the need for a particular outcome, you will increase your chances for success and contentment. It's okay to want and work for a certain outcome; just don't allow your happiness to be entirely contingent on it. Better that your happiness should come from knowing that you gave every attempt your best effort.

Focusing on the process will support your long term confidence. This is not the fleeting sort of confidence that you will succeed in the current attempt, but the self-knowledge that you are on the right path to mastery. You will worry less about the future because you know you will be happy regardless of the outcome of any given situation or event. You'll have more freedom to be spontaneous and take risks. Being unattached to a specific outcome gives you emotional stability when something doesn't turn out the way you had hoped it would. And, the more you focus on process over outcome, the more confident you'll become, and there's nothing more attractive than confidence.

A Strategy for Progress

1. The reward for your persistence and commitment will come as a natural part of your quest for a goal. Focus on the process, aim for continual progress, and stay actively engaged with the present. This is what will lead to success no matter how difficult the goal may be. The reward is the easy part! It will usually take care of itself.

2. Judge your performance on your own terms and in comparison to your own rate of progress. You are the ultimate judge, yet because human beings are social creatures, you will need to resist the very human tendency to worry about what other people might think or say about you in general and your progress in particular. You can't control what other people think and say. It's a pointless waste of energy.

3. Keep everything simple, especially when you are just beginning to learn a new skill or establish a new habit. Effort counts where

talent fails. Effort, in fact, is a better predictor of success than talent or intelligence. Think of every attempt as a preparation for the next attempt, taking advantage of the cascade effect, where every performance builds on the progress of the one before, each attempt getting easier than the last.

4. Think like a winner. Winners concentrate on giving their best to every performance. Judge your performance based on effort rather than outcome. Don't try to win today; try instead to become a winner. Be happy when your best effort results in defeat, not when a weak effort results in victory. Imagine what your best effort would look like, then make it happen.

5. Bring awareness to your performance, either during or immediately afterwards, so you can learn to recognize bad results that follow good processes and vice-versa. With practice you will build the necessary confidence to avoid second-guessing yourself when the results are bad but your technique is good.

CONTROL

My life didn't please me...so I created a new life.
—Coco Chanel

Control is something you do directly or indirectly that results in or causes a reaction or behavior to occur in someone or something else. Self-control is the power to direct or choose your own thoughts and behavior. For example, once you reach the age of 18 you are legally, physically, and morally in control of your own life.

As an adult, it is your responsibility to recognize the difference between two fundamental conditions in your environment: things that are beyond your control, and things that are within your control. You cannot decide or determine what others do, but you can control your own actions and the choices you make in response to others. Once you are able to identify what is not in your control, you can stop wasting time and energy and choose instead to focus on things you can control and in making appropriate decisions that guide you towards your objective.

Bill Bellichick, coach for the New England Patriots, has a sign posted in the team locker room. "Eliminate the noise." That's it. That's all the sign says. His players know exactly what those three words mean, and it's not an admonition to keep the locker room quiet. The sign is there to remind the team to pay attention to the media and to what they say in an interview. The sign is there to remind them that bad talk gives bad results. For example, if a player from the Patriots says something negative about another team, they have given the other team fuel for the next game because all those articles with bad talk in them are put up in the opposing team's locker room before a game and used as motivation against the Patriots. So Bellichick now makes sure his players get the message from day one to stay humble during interviews. It is their actions, their performance on the field, that does most of the talking instead. And judging from his record of wins, it is tough to argue with his method.

What would happen if you learned to "Eliminate the Noise" from your day to day activities? What would change for the better? Try this challenge for one week—just five days—by setting aside the mental junk at least until the weekend. This means turning off the TV and not reading the newspaper for five days. Walk away from the office gossip. How much positive energy would you gain by tuning out the noise in things like "somebody died, there was a robbery, an earthquake somewhere ..." you get the point.

I'm not advocating that you lose your compassion for others or your interest in world affairs, just a change in mindset while you work on your goals and improve your life. If you want to help others or give back to your community, great! Donate your time to a non-profit group or become actively involved in a cause you believe in. You'll be a better person for it. Just be aware of the information that is feeding into your head every day and keep the noise down.

If you read the introduction you were reminded that habits can be good, bad, or anything in between. Some of you will frequently get into the habit of things that are either a waste of energy or a waste of time. Sometimes you will get into a habit that doesn't help in any way at all but simply because it is easier for the moment to be lazy. I call this kind of lazy or unproductive habit a creative avoidance activity. We may think it's easier to get out of doing something by coming up with an excuse or just ignoring it altogether rather than do something more productive. This sort of thinking needs to be challenged because it is based on the false assumption that more effort is required to perform a positive action than a negative one. I firmly believe it is much easier in the long run to do something positive.

Consider television, for example. To be sure, there are some great programs on TV, lots of entertaining, educational, fun stuff. There's also an excess of mindless garbage. With cable providers now offering more than a thousand channels, just the act of flipping through each channel one by one can be a habit all by itself. Just think, you can unlock the potential in your DVR by channel surfing to your heart's desire while simultaneously recording every single episode of Oprah's Super Soul Sunday! Yee-ha! Dial it down, people. Be more selective in your choices, even everyday things like watching TV. Making these little changes will add up to a big difference, a difference that adds meaning and fulfillment to your life.

Instead of passive television watching, why not spend some time engaged in learning a whole new skill set that will benefit you more. Techniques like visualization and positive thinking have long been used by professional athletes to improve their performance and build successful habits, but you don't need to be an athlete to use these same techniques to your own advantage.

Nine Essential Mental Skills

You know the value and effectiveness in creative visualization and positive self-talk. These are great skills on their own and when combined with consistent practice of the actions necessary to achieve your goals, well, your success potential increases accordingly. There's more. The Ohio Center for Sports Psychology has found that athletes are able to increase their performance level significantly when they master a set of nine mental skills. These athletes had such dramatic results that I believe these skills are too good not to share. Even better, the nine skills that follow can be learned by anyone with a little bit of practice.

1.   Goals
Set realistic goals that are high enough to be challenging. Use variety to keep your level of interest high by setting both long-term and short-term goals that are realistic and measurable. Know your current performance level so you can develop specific, detailed plans for improvement. Stay committed to your goals and to the daily process of working towards them.

2.   Imagery

Use creative visualization or positive imagery to train your brain. Prepare for success by imagining yourself being successful. Create and use mental images that are detailed, specific, and realistic. Use imagery to recover from mistakes and failures.

3.   Self Talk

Eliminate negative self-talk and external noise. Maintain your self-confidence through challenging times with positive self-talk. Talk to yourself the way you would talk to your own best friend. Practice using positive self-talk to regulate your thoughts, feelings, and behaviors.

4.   Attitude

Take control of your attitude and choose to be positive. Attitude is a choice. You can choose to be negative or positive but the only attitude that facilitates success is positive. Pursue excellence, not perfection, respecting yourself and the process along the way. Respect these things in others.

5.   Motivation

Keep your motivation level high. Be clear about your motivations and the rewards you expect to achieve. Be patient. There are times when the reward does not come quickly and sometimes the reward is earned from your participation rather than the outcome.

6.   Failure

Learn how failure can move you forward. Accept it. Failure is part of the process and can even be the very thing that moves us forward. Know that some degree of fear can help you perform well and devise an effective strategy to reduce fear when it becomes too strong.

7.   Focus

Stay focused and fearless. Know what you have to pay attention to in a given situation. Learn methods that will keep you focused and that help you resist both internal and external distractions. Know how to restore your focus when you lose concentration.

8.   Communication

Use open communication to build effective, meaningful relationships. People are social beings, which means you are part of a larger system that includes your family, friends, and others. When appropriate, communicate your thoughts, feelings, and needs to these people and be an attentive listener for them as well. Learn the skills for dealing effectively and fairly with conflict, difficult opponents, and other people when they are negative or oppositional.

9.   Confidence

Strengthen your confidence and belief in yourself. Accept strong emotions such as excitement, anger, and disappointment as part of life. Practice using these emotions to improve, rather than interfere with a high level of performance.

Using Mental Skills to Improve Performance

The nine essential mental skills are useful in a wide variety of performance-based situations. Performance-based situations are defined by the following characteristics: they are often scheduled in advance with a set beginning and end; the rules and the participants are known, but not necessarily the outcome. You can, however, effect the outcome, and with preparation before the event, the effect should be a positive one.

An example of a performance-based situation is a job interview. Here are several more examples: taking a driver's test at the DMV, testifying before a judge, giving a sales presentation, participating in a webinar, attending a class reunion, being on a committee, and hosting a play date. Each of these situations and many more like them represent opportunities to apply your skills for a positive outcome.

Every day is a new opportunity to do something that makes a difference in your life, to make a positive change. The actions you take today hold the potential to make tomorrow better than yesterday. Remember, it's okay to look at your past just make it quick. To focus on the past is to risk getting stuck in what seems the easier path of giving in to mistakes or making excuses rather than making progress. "But you don't understand ... Have you any idea what I've had to go through?" I don't buy it and you shouldn't either. Think about this: we seem to regret the things we could have done but didn't, much more than we regret anything we tried to do but failed to achieve.

Consider Thomas Edison. As the story goes, he made more than two thousand attempts to invent an electric lightbulb with a filament that would last. When he was asked about these failed attempts, Edison replied that they were not failures. He had produced, instead, more than two thousand documented ways of how *not* to make a light bulb. He was so determined to solve the problem of the short-lived filament that he was willing to continue working out a solution even after thousands of unsuccessful attempts. Each failure helped to bring him closer to his goal than he was before, until he finally accomplished what he had set out to do.

Success comes in any imaginable shape or size. It can take a lifetime of trial and error, or, if it just so happens to be a day when all is as it should be, (and if we're very, very lucky), victory will be ours on the very first try. Sometimes one win can provide the inspiration for many others to follow as it did with Roger Bannister, the athlete who set his sights on breaking the 4-minute-mile barrier. It was once thought to be physically impossible for a man to run a mile in less than 4 minutes, that is until Bannister broke that barrier in 1954 (Wikipedia, 2014). Then something miraculous happened. Later that same year, other athletes broke the 4-minute record and more soon followed. Today, Bannister's record has become the performance standard for all male runners.

Success. If you think you can, you're right. If you think you can't, you're still right. Why would you choose *not* to be on your own side? After all, isn't that the winner's side?

I'd like to see each one of you believe in yourself and your ability to be successful. The unfortunate reality is that some people don't yet have the confidence or belief in themselves and may be thinking about giving up before they even get started. Don't do it. At the very least, wait until you have given yourself every opportunity to shine.

You know that success often involves a series of mistakes before that critical break-through is made or a milestone achieved. Sometimes it can take years to happen. (Remember all the years it took Jim Carrey.) For many people the difference between giving up and persisting through the toughest times can be a few words of advice from someone who has done it before, and being wise enough to listen.

The best career advice ever given to Scott Adams, creator of the syndicated cartoon Dilbert, were the words "Don't give up." For investor Mark Cuban, that advice came from his dad who taught him that there are no shortcuts. For Lululemon founder Chip Wilson, it was the realization that people actually enjoy helping others. Be open to the advise given by your mentors and those who have accomplished what you are striving to achieve.

PRACTICE

Repetition is the mother of skill.
—Tony Robbins

Practice is the repeated performance of something for the purpose of acquiring a skill, or it can refer to a condition arrived at by experience or exercise. Practice is also used as a synonym for the words habit and custom, or it can be used as a descriptive word for the action or process of performing a routine. With habit replacement, practice is a verb that means specifically fine tuning one's craft by repeating the actions necessary to achieve a goal or desired outcome.

The repetition of an action has a surprisingly similar effect on the brain when compared to visualizing an action: both signal the brain to begin mapping a new neural pathway for the action being practiced by the body or imagined in the mind. The more you practice, the stronger the connections become that make up the pathway. Keep up the practice until the new pathway becomes permanent and the foundation is established for a new habit.

Continued repetition over time will build on the foundation transforming it into a bonafide new habit.

(Incidentally, in the case of visualization, new neural pathways correspond to an image of reality, whereas practice of a physical action will establish pathways that have a physical model. But remember, as far as we can tell, the brain processes the *image* of the physical and the *actual* physical in the same way. It does not seem to distinguish between the two. This may explain, in part, why stroke and accident victims can sometimes achieve a degree of recovery from paralysis.)

There are literally hundreds of automatic behaviors—or habits—that we rely on every day. Some are as simple as putting the cap back on the tube of toothpaste after brushing your teeth, while others are just a little more involved and require more than one decision, like getting dressed or cooking a pot of spaghetti. Still others are activities that are so complicated, it's hard to believe we can do them with barely a thought.

Take any sport, hobby, or activity that you do on a fairly regular basis and picture yourself going through all the steps you take to perform that activity. There's a heck of a lot going on at one time and you don't even know half of it. If your sport is softball or baseball, imagine stepping up to the plate and everything you do and think from that moment on: waiting for the pitch and deciding whether or not to swing; if you swing, did you hit the ball, and if you did, which way did it go? Should you run? If you do and you make it safely to first base, take a quick look around. Where's the ball? Can you get to second base or should you stay at first? Watch the next pitch. Pay attention to the catcher. Maybe you can steal second. These are just the obvious decisions. There are many more going on at the same time. Most of these decisions and all the actions that follow each one have to happen automatically or you won't stay in the game for long. All of this happens out of habit.

The process is essentially the same for any routine behavior. Once the brain identifies the cue for a routine it has stored away in memory (in this case, picking up the bat), the brain's autopilot takes over and runs the routine, freeing the rest of the brain to think other thoughts or to join in on the routine.

As far as we know, habits have played the role of an evolutionary advantage in our survival.

The human brain has learned to favor choices that conserve energy, a life-sustaining function from the earliest years of human history, a time when food was scarce and acquiring it would have been an energy draining activity. Our brains are obligingly happy to make just about any routine behavior into a habit because habits make efficient use of available energy and space. The value in this highly efficient brain of ours can be seen in the freedom we have to think lofty thoughts and the ability to come up with imaginative solutions to any challenge that confronts us.

The ability to conserve mental effort is not without its faults. If our brain should power down at the wrong moment, we could fail to notice something important like that predator over there lurking in the bushes, or that speeding car headed straight at us as we enter an intersection. As a way to bump the odds in our favor, the brain has developed a system that helps it determine if and when it's safe to let a particular habit take over.

Research with rats can demonstrate how this system works (Duhigg, 2014). A group of rats were trained to run through a maze while tiny electrodes recorded their brain activity. Researchers noticed three spikes in the rat's brain activity: the first occurring at the start of the maze, another spike each time a researcher made a clicking sound at strategic points along the route, and a third spike at the moment the rat reached the end of the maze where a chocolate reward was waiting. As it turns out, those spikes were markers of the brain's decision to hand over the controls for behavior to a specific habit. Unable to see beyond the walls of a maze, it would be difficult for a rat to know whether it was secure inside a safety zone, or in a scary and unfamiliar cupboard with a hungry cat on the prowl close by. To cope with this uncertainty, the brain spends a lot of effort looking for a hint (or trigger) that signals a behavior pattern it should use. In this case, the trigger comes in the form of a sound. If the rat hears a click, it knows to go with the maze habit. If it hears a cat's meow, it chooses a different pattern. Then, at the end of the activity when the chocolate reward appears, the brain shakes itself awake and checks to make sure everything is safe and sound as expected.

A similar process operates in the human brain as a three-part loop. First, there is a cue, a trigger that tells your brain it's time to switch over to automatic mode and which habit to use. Then the routine (either physical, mental, or emotional), plays itself out. Finally, there is a reward that helps your brain decide whether or not this particular pattern is worth remembering for the future.

The Positive Habit Feedback Loop

Practice over time creates a three part streaming loop that has a trigger or a cue, a specific behavior associated with that trigger, and a reward that reinforces the behavior when it is performed. Every time the loop runs through a full cycle of trigger-behavior-reward, the loop is strengthened and eventually learns to run on its own. Meanwhile, the bond between the trigger and the reward grows stronger until the two become so closely entwined that your brain can no longer imagine the presence of one without that of the other. The resulting pattern is a powerful cycle of desire, anticipation, and reward, the perfect set up for a new habit.

Habits are maintained by their feedback loop. And you already know that habits are the brain's autopilot, allowing us to focus on other things. Sometimes this automation can be so strong that you have to be relentless in the fight to overcome it and unless you replace it with a new habit, the old one will continue to kick in automatically.

104

Habits have another unnerving talent you should prepare for: they can hide. In one study rats were trained to repeatedly run through a maze until reaching the end without a wrong turn became a habit. Then they put a stop to the habit by changing the reward. Later on, researchers put the reward back in its original place and to their surprise, the rats performed the old habit without missing a beat. Maybe there's some truth to that familiar phrase, "once you learn to ride a bike, you'll never forget how." It seems that old habits never disappear completely (Alexander, 2013).

This might seem like a major obstacle to overcoming negative behavior, but habits may be so persistent because this was an evolutionary advantage. Imagine the problems if you had to relearn things like the routine aspects of your job after every weekend off, or if your kids had to find their way to school as if for the first time after every spring and summer break. The downside is that the human mind plays no favorites when it comes to bad versus good habits. To your brain, they're the same. So, if you have conquered a bad habit, be aware that it's really just hibernating, ready to jump back in to the fray when the conditions are right.

This explains in part why it is so hard to establish long term exercise routines or to change what we eat. If our habit is to sit in front of the TV during dinner, that pattern will stick inside our heads. On the other hand, if we learn to create new routines that overpower the unwanted behavior—that is, if we take deliberate measures to interrupt the feedback loop—we can force those bad habits into the background. And once we create a new pattern overlay, say going for a walk right after dinner, it will become as automatic as any other habit.

Habits help to keep our brains quietly humming along. We know that without the energy conserving function of our habits, our brains would shut down, overwhelmed by the minutiae of daily life. Certain types of brain injuries and diseases can leave a person in a state of mental paralysis that interferes with the performance of everyday activities like opening a door or deciding what to eat. They may lose the ability to ignore what we usually consider to be insignificant details—for example, they cannot recognize facial expressions, including fear and disgust, because they don't know what to focus on. With an injured brain, access to the hundreds of habits we rely on is lost, habits that include the way we handle any number of tiny details and everyday decisions that make our lives easier and more productive. Were you delayed this morning while you tried to remember how to put your shoes and socks on? Did you have to stop to figure out if you should use a fork or a spoon to eat your cereal with?

Of course not. Those decisions are trouble free habits. As long as your brain is healthy and the cues remain constant, these familiar routines will continue to kick in right when they are supposed to. It should be just as easy for you to interpret the facial expressions of the people you see throughout the day.

What about the way you see yourself? Your self image is important to your confidence and to your ability to interact effectively with others. For good or bad, the way we act towards others is a reflection of the way we see ourselves. If our self image is high, for example, the tendency is for us to expect to be treated with respect and fairness, which are the same standards we use to treat others. If our self-image is low, our relationships with others will be adversely effected. The good news is that we can make positive changes if our self image is one that does not support our goals. The act of achieving a goal (even a simple one) can start the process of positive change. There is nothing better for your self image than having some successes under your belt.

In major league baseball the best hitter has a batting average of 330 while an average hitter has a batting average of 260. The difference works out to be 7 more hits per 100 times at the plate. Doesn't sound like much does it? But it also works out to a difference of several million dollars per player.

Of course, both are great baseball players. Both are in great shape. But I can guarantee that the one who hits 330 is the one who sees himself as a better hitter. Yet that very same 330 hitter fails twice as much as he succeeds. He just doesn't let that thought stick around in his head. He can't afford it. He would not have a 330 average if he did. It really is that simple.

Think about this. These guys play baseball almost every day during the season. They take batting practice before every game, and some of them even practice on their day off. If you want to be the best at what you do, then you have to practice too. Your self image, just like everything else, is a habit. You have a habitual way of thinking about yourself, and, for better or worse and like any other habit, if it's not serving you well, change it so it does.

The Bumble Bee Revisited

The front edge of the pitcher's plate is 18 inches behind the center of the mound, making the front edge's midpoint at 60 feet, 6 inches from the rear edge of home plate. Six inches in front of the pitcher's plate, the mound begins to slope downward in a straight shot towards home.

That's how far the pitcher has to throw the ball to land in the catcher's mitt, 60 feet, 6 inches, or better yet, that's how far the batter has to wait to react and hit the ball. That's right. Like the bumble bee story, it sounds impossible. A ball roughly 3 inches in diameter, airborne and moving at an average speed of 85 to 95 miles per hour, so fast that it takes but a fraction of a second to pass over the spot where the batter stands poised to swing and run in a single fluid motion. The batter has long practiced for this moment, keenly aware that the odds of a hit are against him.

Today's pitchers have at least three to five different pitches: the two-seam fastball, the four-seam fastball, the infamous curve ball, and the slider, a repertoire that leaves the batter guessing at what the pitcher will throw. When he guesses it right, the odds shift slightly in favor that he'll make a hit, proving that baseball is a mix of talent, intuition, experience, and a lot of practice. Because the pitcher invariably has the advantage, when a hitter has a batting average of 330 or better, or has more than 100 runs batted in to home plate (RBIs) in a single season, well, what you've got is baseball's equivalent to the bumble bee, a thing that is truly amazing.

Some people go through life thinking that the odds are stacked against them, that their goals (if they attempt to have any at all), are just too tough. If you think your own goals are too tough, well, you are probably correct. But they are not impossible if you are willing to keep at it. It's possible to achieve amazing things regardless of the odds. Dr. Martin Luther King, Jr. was at first reluctant as he stepped in to lead the modern civil rights movement. Under his 13 year leadership, more progress was made toward racial equality than in the preceding 350 years. As if that alone wasn't achievement enough, he accomplished this while advocating non-violent protest, a method he learned from Gandhi. King was so successful that he started a campaign to end poverty and another to end international unrest, working tirelessly against the odds until his life was cut short by an assassin's bullet. We can only wonder at what more he could have gone on to achieve.

King's life can still inspire us when things get really tough. The person who practices on a regular basis, who shows up every day, works hard, and deals with failure in a constructive way, this is the person who achieves the greatest success. You have to believe in yourself. If you are not working on your attitude and self-image every day, it's time to get started.

ATTITUDE

*Keep your thoughts positive because your
thoughts become your words.
Keep your words positive because your words
become your behavior.
Keep your behavior positive because your
behavior becomes your habits.
Keep your habits positive because your habits
become your values.
Keep your values positive because your values
become your destiny.*
——*Mahatma Gandhi*

Attitude is having a settled way of thinking or feeling about someone or something that is reflected in our actions towards that person or thing. Simple enough, but here's the kick. Behavioral specialists have had a long-standing "chicken or the egg" argument over how our thoughts and feelings are formed. Do our actions shape our attitudes, or is it the other way around, with our attitudes being the source of our actions? I think Gandhi, in the quote above, got it right, and science seems to agree, for the most part. What we do and what we say will have a strong influence in how we think about the object of our words and actions. The next logical question is whether or not we can deliberately change or eliminate an undesirable attitude by changing how we act.

The question is an important one for habit replacement because it points us to the best strategy to optimize results. When your goal is to change an attitude or mindset, your action plan should begin with learning new behaviors that are targeted to change your way of thinking. It is important to keep in mind that the lines separating thought goals from behavior goals are fuzzy. They overlap each other. So do the techniques for achieving those goals. In other words, we can use every tool in the box or a combination of two or three as long as they accomplish the goal.

For example, visualization and affirmations along with consistent practice of physical actions are all great tools for habit replacement because they encourage the brain to map out new neural pathways that establish the foundation for new habits. The general idea here is that we can change our behavior with consistent practice. When the behavior change becomes a routine, our attitude should make the adjustment to fit the new reality, a habit of success.

Now we've just about come full circle. Is it easier to think your way into acting? Or to act your way into thinking? The answer, I believe, should be obvious. You can change (or control) your attitude by first changing your behavior. Remember that habits can be mental as well as physical. Your mental skills need practice just like any other.

Repetition is the key. Like athletes who practice the same pattern of movement over and over again, you also need to practice the behavior pattern that will become a new habit, and then continue to practice in order to maintain and improve your competency. Practice also makes it easier to achieve the expected outcome and lowers the odds of repeating the same mistakes. With enough practice, you will catch yourself thinking about something else at the same time. Have you ever driven home from work and by the time you pull in the driveway, you can't remember how you got there? Now, that's an established habit. When you know a routine this well, you are confident that when it really counts, it will get done right.

Mental skills operate on the same principle as behavior-based skills, only here the goal is to fill your head with the right stuff so there is no room for negative, self-defeating thoughts to find their way in. I call this controlling your environment. For example, imagine that you are driving to work. You have your favorite music playing on the radio. Then there's a breaking bulletin with bad news in between songs. Why not listen to an audio book instead to block out the negative news on the car radio. When you get home, the TV is on. Oh no, more bad news. How about reading something uplifting instead of watching TV. Reading is one of the best things you can do to improve your mental fitness and your overall point of view. Why not spark up those neural connections I keep telling you about and flood your brain with just the positive stuff!

Here is another perspective. Think of attitude as mind control. No, this is not a form of brain washing. It is the fact that you have the choice of making a commitment to control what goes in to your brain and what goes on in your mind, or you can leave the door open and allow someone else do it for you. And that's a truly frightening thought.

Being a success in life doesn't always require originality. More often it depends on mundane things like your attitude towards your job or career, what goals you choose, and how hard you are willing to work to achieve those goals.

It would be fantastic to come up with an original idea that produced an overnight fortune in profits, something like Velcro or Whiteout, but the reality is that success of this kind is rare and fleeting, and besides, it's not a thing you can guarantee just by modeling yourself after those who have already done it. Finding a mentor certainly helps, but this is just one step in a much larger process. You could also try putting in more energy and enthusiasm in what you already do every day. This is another valid step you can take towards a higher level of success. Great. Now you have two steps in a much larger process with many more steps to go. Achieving success is, in a way, like algebra. You won't get points for originality, but when you follow each step carefully, you always wind up with the correct answer. Hey! It's the algebra of success!

Successful Failure

I'm a firm believer in positive thinking and in the idea that failure can move you closer to your goals when your attitude is positive, your mind is open to learning, and change is something you embrace. To me, this is failure done right.

Maybe if we were to start thinking about change differently then failure would lose some of its power to scare us. We only have to look as far as our own bodies to get a glimpse of how this works. The cells in our bodies are constantly changing and being replaced. Case in point, every 5 days all the cells that line the stomach are regenerated. If you have a really bad meal on Monday, by Saturday it's all forgotten (at least from your stomach's point of view), because all the old cells have been replaced with new ones. Every 45 days all the cells of your liver are new; after 90 days, a new skeleton. As the theory goes, in 7 years you should have a brand new body. (Seven years is also the time it takes for a bankruptcy to clear off your credit report ... another way to a whole new you!)

What I'm getting at is not the debate over cellular renewal but the fact that our bodies are automatically set up to maintain a healthy state of being. All we need to do is give it a little help. More to the point, imagine if we did this with our thinking. A bad experience would go the route of those cells lining our stomach and would be replaced. No need to hang on to bad memories, mistakes, and failures beyond recognizing them and learning a lesson perhaps. Then it's time to get on with living.

Fear is the vestige of a primitive, instinctive response to a real or perceived threat. Turning again to our ancient ancestors for an example, fear would have been an important mechanism for survival. The growl of a pissed off hungry bear would have kicked on the brain's fight or flight instinct, sending our ancestors running for safety or throwing a hand axe in defense. Running away was a habitual response to fear and it has persisted to this day. Talk about a stubborn habit!

Today, we continue to live and struggle with our fears. The majority of them—the fear of failure included—have been drilled into our memories where they reside in the corners of the mind until a trigger brings out a defensive response to a perceived threat. The fear of failure is especially irrational with its insidious hold that keeps us from taking intelligent risks that, if we were to at least try, might just be the next step towards a more extraordinary life.

Challenge your fear. Think of fear as an old habit, one that you can now replace with a new way of thinking and a positive view that embraces change.

Positive Mindset
When your attitude is positive and you begin every day in the direction of your goal, you are absolutely certain to get there. It is still possible

to experience a set back or failure despite your best efforts simply because you cannot control every single variable. There are things that you do have control of, such as your attitude and how you react to a failure. For example, what do you do before leaving the house when it looks like it might rain? Maybe you can't accurately predict the weather 100 percent of the time, but you can mitigate the risk by choosing to take along an umbrella.

Here's another way to look at being positive. Try catastrophizing the outcome of a problem or situation. In other words, imagine the most extreme possible consequence of failure. Now compare that to a rational, more likely result if you fail. You'll probably end up somewhere other than where you had planned. It could be a place just as good as where you would be if you did nothing, or it could be worse, or who knows, you just might have a happy accident that puts you somewhere even better.

Do you know how many positive things have happened in this world as a result of a mistake? I can name several off the top of my head: Post it™ notes were a mistake. *Fabreeze*™ fabric freshener was a mistake. The microwave oven? An accidental side effect. Heck, even some of Thomas Edison's one thousand patented inventions were the unintentional consequences of a failure. You can attract all sorts of neat stuff when your attitude is right. It's like being a cool stuff magnet. Maybe you could be a new super hero, the great *Magnattractor*, master of a universe that is helpless to resist the attraction of your positivity. It's like the laws of thermodynamics, positive in equals positive out. There are very strict rules of physics at play that can't be stopped. Why not use them to your advantage!

People often tell me that I have it easier than they do, that I'm always positive and upbeat and they wish they had been born naturally positive like I was. Hello, people! We are all born positive. If you are acting negative, well, that's exactly right—you're acting. You have practiced, drilled, rehearsed, and performed the role you play in life. But guess what. It's time to change characters. Go back to being like a child. Even JC himself says so in the Bible.

What, exactly, does it mean to go back to being like a child? In one word: enthusiasm. With life or with the god-like force within you. Sense that you are alive. Be with life in the present moment. Participate. If you are not enthusiastic now, what does that say about how you will feel on the day you die? Does the notion of regret come to mind? That doesn't sound like it can be a good thing at all.

Okay, I can hear some of you accusing me of just taking a bunch of words and using them to my advantage. Guilty! That's exactly what I'm doing and you can do the same thing. It's a positive move. Remember, words can be powerful. It's no exaggeration to say that wars have been fought over them. Why not use words instead to send a positive message to others.

I prefer to control my environment, both mentally and physically. I read and I listen to positive, inspirational recordings every chance I have. At the gym, in the car, at home, every morning, every day. If I don't do this I risk handing over the power to control my environment (and my life), to someone else. And I might not like what someone else plans to do with me.

Pay attention to your immediate environment. Are you allowing the negative in the world to control you? Even a thing as simple as what you listen to can mean the difference in whether or not you determine your own environment and your own attitude. For those who are stubborn about the need to hear what is going on in the world, trust me, you will continue to hear the news you feel you need to hear from the people you come in contact with throughout the day. Let that be enough for awhile and see if it makes a difference or not.

A few more words about the law of attraction, something that works in your favor only when it is followed by the law of action. You cannot just sit at home and visualize your life the way you want it to be and expect anything to change. Thinking alone does not make it so. Yes, visualization and meditation are extremely important as tools. But they have to be teamed up with a positive attitude and actions that are consistent with your goals. This is the trifecta—Imagine Positive Action—it's the law of attraction meets the law of action!

BECOME A STUDENT OF LIFE

Everyone you will ever meet knows something you don't.
– Bill Nye "the science guy"

A student in the traditional sense is a person who studies at a school or college; someone who studies in order to enter a particular profession. Now I'm going to stretch the boundaries of grammar. If the word student was a verb, how would the definition change? Then a student would mean a person who is dedicated to life-long learning; someone who never believes they have arrived, thus putting an end to their journey. Instead, they are "sharpening the ax" for the next challenge, always eager to learn and discover more. For the student of life, graduation only comes on the day they die.

Being a student of life is an advantage to building positive habits and goals. People have a natural curiosity and ability to change that will have many of you looking for new ways to do things and new experiences to try. You become a better person for it. Here's how it works.

125

The Zen of YouTube

Now, I'm not suggesting that you can attain nirvana on YouTube, even though we know it can help with guided meditation. There's just a lot more to YouTube than those crazy viral videos that entertain us. I think of it as a free access, on demand university with an instant digital library that covers virtually any topic you can think of. Let's take a walking tour of how you can add YouTube to your goal-achieving tool kit. Let's say you have decided to work on three major goals over the next 12 months.

Your first big target is to lose weight and get healthy. Start by preparing the way for success. Get educated. Buy three books that appeal to you on the subject of losing weight and/or getting healthy and then make a commitment to cover a certain amount of reading every day. Let's say this will be 20 pages. You can read more, but never less. Go ahead and make this a fun task, especially if you don't like to read. As an alternative or just to add some variety, go online and browse YouTube for an audio-video you can relate to. Try typing "get healthy now" in the search bar and see what you can find.

When it comes to being healthy I'm a big fan of physical exercise. To keep things interesting I change my workout every 60 days. I go to

YouTube and type in, let's say, chest workout. I watch a few videos that are different from what I'm currently doing, find one I like, watch it several times, and write down the steps. Now I have my workout for the next 60 days. Then I go back to my workout and do the same thing! I also combine chest and triceps (pushing), and back and biceps (pulling), and then on day three, it's legs and shoulders. To sum it all up, day one: chest and triceps; day two: back and biceps; day three: legs and shoulders. Then I start all over again. It's fun mixing it up and starting a whole new routine every 60 days. I also swim four days a week after my weight workout. I have been doing this for years. The benefits are so positive that they flow into every other aspect of my life. I couldn't imagine living without a workout routine. It's definitely a habit.

If this kind of thing is all new for you, I strongly recommend that you start with a trainer like I did, at least for the first few months. A trainer can help you get the maximum results and the most benefit while tailoring your routine to your personal abilities and goals. Some people enjoy using a personal trainer so much that they always have one. Do whatever works for you!

Now, let's say your second goal is to earn more money. Do the same thing! Pick three or four books on the subject and do a search on YouTube. There are so many great speeches and seminars to choose from. It's crazy. Heck, you can even get *Think and Grow Rich* by Napoleon Hill free online. Another great classic available online is *The Power of Positive Thinking* by Norman Vincent Peale. You will be happily surprised by the number of interesting reads you can find at no cost on the internet, not only on YouTube. Check out the digital books and videos at the following online libraries:

Project Guttenberg
http://www.archive.org

Bartleby's classic literature and reference works
http://www.bartleby.com/

Open Library
http://www.openlibrary.com

Your third major goal is to cultivate spirituality. Do the same here as for the first two. By now you can see that even if you don't have a lot of money to spare, you can get well into this journey as long as you have a computer or a smart phone—or even just a library card. There is no excuse to keep you from getting started.

Except you! The real question to ask yourself is whether you are ready and willing to change. How much do you want these positive things in your life?

To continue our walk-through, choose your most important goals and break them down into learning events. Become a student of each one and have at it. The pay off is this: it's very fulfilling and a heck of a lot of fun to advance every day in the direction of your goals. You will feel like you are doing all that you can on that particular day. What a great feeling! A word of caution: try not to take on too much at one time. Three or four goals at once is enough. Get those down and then move on to the next.

In addition to learning all you can about your specific goals, you also have to learn to be persistent each and every day. There is no such thing as losing or not achieving your goal as long as you don't quit. The key is having the persistence to keep moving forward even if you make a mistake, even if it takes more time than you thought it would, even if fear or anxiety causes you to stumble or stall. Keep moving forward! How do you learn to be more persistent? Try the following strategy.

Five Point Strategy to Stay in the Game

1. Your goal has to be worth it, otherwise what's the point of doing the work? One of the original success authors, Napoleon Hill, would say that you have to have a burning desire. Desire provides the incentive that will carry you through those days when little progress is made, yet still leaves you with enough drive to get up the next day and do the work all over again. You endure the down side of the process—and you can count on there being a down side—because the goal is worth it.

2. Your written action plan, much like a business plan, will strengthen your commitment by sending a message to your subconscious mind that this is serious work for an important goal. It adds fuel to your positive habit feedback loop.

3. The benefit of any new skill or behavior is only fully realized when you reach a level of competency in that skill. Competency is a payoff in itself when you practice consistently.

4. Focus on eliminating negative self talk. This can be especially tough towards the end of the day when you are more likely to feel

tired. Reserve some energy for silencing the chatter. Keep your thoughts positive. Don't give up before the miracle happens!

5. Learn from other successful people who have accomplished some of things that you are now working towards. This is not rocket science. Don't be afraid to ask for help or advice. Where it's appropriate, model your own behavior after those who have achieved goals that are similar to yours.

Keeping it Simple

Trying to complicate this deal is simply creative avoidance!
–Rick Berube

Success is more likely when both the goal and the plan to attain it are clear and specific. Have you ever tried to follow the directions that came packaged with a piece of furniture you bought at Ikea? How long did it take you to figure it out? Were you left thinking there had to be an easier way? Does your brain hurt yet? Complicated is exhausting. Simplicity, defined as having the condition or state of being that is easy to understand or do, just makes sense, especially when you expect to have the energy level it takes to build a new habit.

Sometimes simplicity gets confused with stupidity—but as much as it might be tempting to do so, simplicity is the absence of *complexity*, not the absence of intelligence. I make this point in order to avoid confusion, which, as it turns out, is often what results from something made to be more complicated than it needs to be.

A complicated or unclear goal is not just difficult to work with. It also provides a ready-made reason to quit for those who are "commitophobic," people who have trouble enough with change let alone the demands of replacing a habit. The temptation exists for some of us to make the process of achieving a goal more difficult than it actually is or needs to be, so that doing nothing becomes an easier outcome to digest. Put another way, we are more receptive to changing our behavior and more likely to attain success when our goals and actions are simple, specific, and very clear.

Enough said. Let's take a closer look at the advantages in keeping things simple. Imagine if you tried to quench your thirst by taking a drink from a fire hose. You might succeed in nearly drowning yourself, but little else. A fire hose is clearly too much for the goal. Break it down into something simple instead. Try manageable, reasonable steps like go find a faucet and fill up a cup. Now the odds shift in your favor that you will achieve a satisfying drink of water. I've chosen an extreme example to point out an important idea, that you can break down a major task into manageable chunks that allow you to successfully take on an otherwise overwhelming challenge. You have effectively turned a big problem into a series of small hurdles.

There's a clear advantage to working with several simple targets spread out over a period of time rather than attempting one gigantic goal at once. From your current perspective relative to that single huge goal, you may have to make an equally huge leap, a leap that puts you at a high risk of falling. Why make things harder on yourself than they have to be? Keep it simple. Break down a complex goal into smaller, more manageable chunks that reward you sooner and lessen the chance of defeat. Remember, every time you establish a new behavior that replaces an old one, the new builds on the progress of the one before, making it easier for you to change the next behavior. If you make a mistake along the way, don't worry. It's a shorter fall. Get up and try again.

It's easy to get caught up in the business of living, nerves frazzled by competing obligations and an endless To Do list. Add to the mix one or two unexpected emergencies (because, let's face it, for some people the drama of an occasional emergency is all the excitement they get), and you can convince yourself that your bad habits really aren't all that bad. Just keep doing things the same way as before and hang on to the hope for a different, better outcome. Right?

Wrong! Oh sure, you can convince yourself that you don't have any harmful habits, at least for today. Trust me. They'll be there ready to take over when your guard is down. Bad habits will trip you up and snag your dreams and you won't even know it until after the dust has cleared. You deserve better. Don't hold yourself down or invite a dead-end struggle by complicating things. Here's a short list of tips to help you keep the journey simple.

The Short List

1. Focus on progress not perfection.
2. Take progressive steps. Measure today's success against yesterday's performance rather than tomorrow's goal.
3. Failure is a signal to work harder and smarter, not an excuse to give up.
4. Break it down. Turn one complicated goal into a series of smaller achievable goals.
5. Small changes add up to BIG results.

Each new day is an opportunity to renew your commitment, to build on your success, to lose the need to get hung up on yesterday's issues. Keep it simple and each day will get easier than the last. Imagine waking up every morning to a clean slate with the freedom to go any direction you please. This is your day. What you make of it is up to you.

This should be easy to understand: there are no bonus points awarded for over-complicating things. Have you ever received a failing grade in school because your report needed to be more complicated? Probably not. How about a boss who demanded that there be more noise and confusion in the office? Not very likely. Keep it simple. Make this the principle that organizes your day.

A Few Key Ideas

Responsibility: Take responsibility for your thoughts, words, and actions. That whole sentence is really a decision in disguise. It's your choice. When you wake up in the morning, what are you going to think about? What actions are you going to take? Positive thoughts and positive actions! Make the effort until "positivity" becomes natural and automatic.

Belief: Commit to your goal. Say it out loud with power and conviction. If you want to lose 25 pounds, tell yourself at least a few times a day "I weigh 25 pounds less!" If your occupation is in sales and you want to close 50 deals, make it a daily affirmation: "I will close 50 deals." If you want to earn $200,000, same thing. "I earn $200,000 a year!" By the way, don't neglect your mental GPS. Be sure of your destination and how you plan to get there.

Consistency: Make your daily actions consistent with your goals. Every day you have two choices. You can use your energy to do your job and feel great about it, or you can use your energy to kick the crap out of yourself and feel miserable with guilt for not doing your job.

You are smart. If you are being inconsistent, you will know it, and even though it's natural to be tough on yourself, stop it this instant. Take it one day at a time. Yesterday is good for its educational value and tomorrow may never come. Make the most of today's activities.

Focus: Emphasize the process rather than the outcome and success will take care of itself. If you choose to focus on the outcome instead, you are either complacent, desperate, or overly competitive. A more productive approach is to focus on the process, measuring your progress by a comparison of your performance over time. Competition becomes uplifting and fun when it takes the form of a challenge, not a smack down. Its simple. Believe in the process and the goals you have committed to.

Mind Control: Realize you can't control everything that happens around you. You can only control you. This one is really tough. Keep the blinders on when it comes to the distraction of negative noise. Turn down the volume.

Never stop working on your mental skills. Read, read, read ... or listen to audio books. Always have one of these going in your car. Make this one of your top priorities!

Practice: Much like my advice for reading, you have to practice, practice, and practice some more. You have to keep at it every day until you've mastered the action, and it doesn't stop there. In order to keep a skill at its peak or to maintain a habit (yes, even habits need maintenance), continue to practice on a daily basis.

Life-long Learning: Learn something new each day. Fearlessly explore new ideas and opposing views. Cultivate an open mind and the whole world will be yours. Learn a new, more productive habit in place of that old negative one.

Success: This is not some random event that with any luck, will happen to you ... or not. If this were true, you might as well be waiting around for never. Success is something you plan for and build on every day through your actions and your thoughts.

Creative Avoidance

As you can see, there is nothing inherently complicated about being successful and trying to make it that way is simply a creative avoidance activity. In other words, you are the one causing the distraction that is preventing your progress in the direction you say you want to go. Seriously. Stop getting in your own way! Once you make the decision and the commitment, it's time to act. If that action results in an initial fail, it's okay. Fail forward. There is no such thing as absolute perfection. Set your aim for progress!

Learning a new way of thinking or acting, and unlearning an old pattern is just as challenging as it is exciting, but it should never be complicated. Habit replacement therapy seeks to make these changes easier so that success is the natural outcome.

Whether your goal is to break a bad habit, to build a new one, or to accomplish both, the process can be summarized in three simple words:

Plan, Prepare, Practice

Everything else is an elaboration of these three core principals. When you make a decision and commit to a plan, take steps to prepare and then implement the consistent actions that put your plan in motion, you will have a unique system to maximize your potential as well as your success. Keep it simple!

THE FINISH LINE

Win as if you were used to it; lose as if you enjoyed it for a change.
—Ralph Waldo Emerson

Here you are at the home stretch! If you haven't set a goal and written a plan yet, be sure to grab a pen and paper and get started as soon as you finish reading this chapter. You have a great set of tools to conquer your first bad habit by putting a positive one in its place. As you start the quest to make every day a success, use the ideas and strategies described in the following pages to strengthen your resolve. Some of these strategies will be a review of what you already know, while others will be entirely new. There's always something more to learn, always a higher level you can reach, always a new challenge waiting on the far side of your current goal. As long as you have a pulse, you have the power to build a better life. Write me an email to let me know how you're doing. I'll be here cheering you on!

Getting Prepared

One habit at a time:
Especially if this is your first experience. Changing your behavior and breaking a habit is hard enough. Don't chase after failure by taking on more than one or two changes at a time. If the behavior or habit you want to change is something big, you can break it down into smaller goals that are easier to work with. After you've accomplished a few simple changes, you can take on greater challenges, but always stick to one or two goals at a time. This will give you the best chance of success.

Break it down:
Your first few goals should be as simple as you can make them so that your efforts are sure to be successful. You can even think of these as warm ups before the real thing. Early success provides a priceless boost to your confidence that could mean the difference between crossing the finish line or giving up altogether. Start small and with a narrow focus. Is your goal to start an exercise routine? Start with 5 or 10 minutes and gradually increase your time to 30 minutes. Do you need to wake up earlier? Get in the habit of waking up 10 minutes earlier first and then set another goal, adding on 10

minutes more and so on. Eventually you will reach your ultimate target.

Know your reason why:
Be very clear about your reasons for wanting to change. What are both the short and the long-term benefits? Are there people who will share in the good that will come from your success, making the goal even more worthwhile? Solid reasons and a clear purpose will improve the likelihood of forward momentum. When the time comes to write down your action plan, state clearly the reasons for choosing specific goal and include the people (such as your spouse or children), who will share the benefits of your success. This will finalize your commitment to them as well as to yourself.

Be patient:
It takes a minimum of 30 days to change a habit under ideal circumstances and with a simple goal, but realistically, the average is closer to 60 days. This means you must stay focused and consistent for that amount of time. Of course, some people and some habits will take more time, others less. Sixty days however, is an average that seems to fit most people most of the time, so give yourself at least that much time in the beginning. Make a commitment and *do not give up* even if you experience a set back.

Make a firm commitment:
Make a commitment to your goal and say it out loud. It's also good practice to visualize yourself achieving your goal. Yet even when you do both, stating and imagining your goal, your commitment needs to be stronger. Just saying you'll do it is not enough. Make it as serious as a contract by writing it down on paper. If you want to quit smoking, write the words "I will quit smoking" on paper. If you want to keep your desk organized, write "I will keep my desk organized."

Build a support system:
Make a list of the people in your life who you can turn to if you need advice and emotional support. Talk to them about your plans and ask for their continued support as you work towards your goals. Include their names and contact information in your written plan so you will have it readily on hand. If your habit is one that has reached the level of addiction, find a local support group or online forum and make use of this important resource. (See the appendix at the end of this book for contact information of the largest of these support groups.)

Devise a strategy:
We all run in to roadblocks along the way to our goals. Many are easy to work around with some

146

advance planning, while others can be more of a problem. Don't wait for these to reach your doorstep. Take the time now to figure out if there are any potential roadblocks you might encounter and what you can do to overcome them. A little planning today means you will be better prepared tomorrow and more successful in the long-run.

Identify your triggers:
Ask yourself what triggers the habit you want to change. There might be only one, but for most habits, there are several situations, people, or places that initiate the behavior. If you are a smoker, for example, your triggers could be having a coffee, finishing dinner, taking a break from work, and so on. Identify all of them and include this in your written plan.

Create an escape route:
No, this is not a quitting plan. This is your plan of escape when you run into a trigger. A trigger is like a dinner bell calling you to your bad habit. For every trigger, decide on a positive behavior to replace the negative one that is set off by the trigger. When you first wake up in the morning, instead of smoking a cigarette, what will you do? Do you go out for a drink every Friday after work? Instead, make Friday the day you wash your car or go for a walk.

Put it in writing:
This is where you'll take the commitment you made and all the strategies you've worked out, and turn them into a systematic plan of action. This plan does not need to be complicated. It can be as simple as a single sentence statement of your goal with a bullet list of actions, or something that goes into greater detail. The key is to get a plan in writing using a format that makes sense to you and then keep this written plan close at hand either posted on a wall or carried in a pocket as a daily reminder of the benefit in seeing your plan through to completion.

Choose a start date:
Grab a calendar and choose a specific date to get started that is at least a week or two in the future. Habit change is important. Give it the attention and preparation time worthy of such an endeavor and you will be rewarded with success. Let your support people know this date, as well as any others who are willing to be a positive resource. Then post your start date where you will see it every morning. Look forward to this as the day you begin the work towards a better life. Make it a day of celebration.

Getting Started

Use your support group:
Enlist the help of the support group that you identified in the planning stages. Remind them of how important this is and that you are counting on them. Remember that you can also take advantage of any organized support groups in your area, especially for help making it through the really tough spots.

Be aware of negative self-talk:
We all talk to ourselves in our head. (And no, responding to yourself does not necessarily mean you're crazy.) Self-talk can be damaging however, if we allow the negative kind to have free range. Start paying attention to the things you tell yourself because this is one way your brain establishes those new connections and pathways that have an impact on your reality. Be aware of any negative self-talk and quickly replace it with a message that supports your goals.

Keep a positive attitude:
You will have negative thoughts. The important thing is that you are able to identify them for what they are and swiftly kick them out of your head with a positive statement. Say something positive out loud if you have to, just don't allow

negative thinking to take up space in your head. Nothing can shut down your efforts to replace a bad habit faster than a negative attitude. In fact, negative thinking in itself can be a bad habit that infects every area of your life like an unwanted houseguest. Kick them out now!

Overcome the impulse:
Impulsive behavior is often unavoidable but if you stick with your plan and give each day your best effort, these impulses will gradually loosen their grip until you can break free from the hold they have on your life. It took time to develop your habits and all the related triggers and behaviors; it will take time to replace them.

Control your environment:
It's inevitable that you will run in to negative people, people who will even try to get you to keep your old habit no matter how harmful it may be. You will always run in to negative background noise like the daily news that can frustrate your efforts to keep a positive outlook. Be ready for it. If it's people, confront them, and be direct with your words. Tell them what you are trying to accomplish and that you need their support. If they persist in undermining your efforts you will have to make the choice not to be around them, and tell them this. If the problem is background noise, turn off the TV or

stop reading the newspaper, at least during the time you are establishing the new habit.

Use daily affirmations:

Be your own cheerleader by giving yourself pep talks. Repeat your mantra or your affirmations either silently or out loud. (Even if a few people get to thinking you've lost your marbles. This is not for their benefit, it's for yours.) Once you've quit smoking or landed that promotion, these people are not going to think you're crazy anymore. They will be too busy feeling like lazy, unhealthy, do-no-goodies.

Picture success:

Remember the power of your mind. Your brain creates the same pathways when you visualize yourself doing something as it does when you actually do that same activity. Creative visualization is one of the most powerful tools you can use to build a new habit. Use it every day to maximize your results.

Reward your progress:

It is a good habit to reward yourself for improved performance and for reaching milestones along the way. Rewards serve to strengthen and reinforce your positive habit feedback loop. Be good to yourself: you've earned it.

One thing at a time:
We know the benefits in taking things one day at a time, of thinking in terms of being responsible to make it through one 24-hour period at a time. There are some situations that need to be broken down even further to the level of the individual impulse or urge. Use the same strategies that apply to the one day at a time approach, except here you just need to make it through one urge at a time.

Keep your actions consistent with your goals:
Why in the world would anyone take the time and energy to set a goal, write up a plan, make a commitment to that plan … and then run around like the Mad Hatter making lots of noise about all these great changes but taking no action to back them up? Don't let that person be you. Your time is much too important, your future too valuable. Say what you mean, mean what you say, and prove it by what you do every day.

Get plenty of sleep:
This is a no-brainer. When you're tired you are at greater risk of a set back. When you regularly deprive yourself of sleep, your body is unable to reset important systems, leading to short term memory loss, an inability to make decisions,

weakened immune responses, cravings for sugar, weight gain, and an all around cranky disposition. Sleep deprivation is going to cause a lot of static in your positive habit feedback loop and this would be a bad thing. Very bad.

Stay hydrated:
This is another no-brainer. Drink plenty of water. Just as a lack of sleep causes all sorts of problems, being dehydrated also leaves us open to failure. Stay hydrated!

Renewal:
Remind yourself often of your commitment, especially at the beginning and end of each day. Read through your plan. Celebrate your success, and reward your milestones. Here's another tip: preparation is an on-going process. When an unexpected obstacle occurs, prepare yourself in case it happens again. Strategize, reformulate, renew. Have some fun and keep things fresh to fight the slumps and down days that are an inevitable part of life.

Accountability:
This is like having responsibility, motivation, and tracking all rolled up into one. Find a mentor, a partner, or a support group who you can report your progress to once a week or once every two weeks. Having to report to

someone—even when it's voluntary—is a strong incentive to stick to your plan.

Build your positive habit feedback loop:
Nothing you do occurs in a vacuum. The more you practice your new behavior, the stronger your performance and the more assured your success will be. Every success will boost your confidence and motivation as well. When you improve one aspect you provide support for the next, forming a continuous loop of positive energy. This positive habit feedback loop contributes to your continued success by making it harder to fail.

Practice positive avoidance:
Not to be confused with creative avoidance, positive avoidance is the deliberate act of staying away from situations that are associated with an old habit. This is the kind of avoidance that makes it easier for you to reach your goal. Practice positive avoidance at least for those critical first few weeks.

Let's say your goal is to quit smoking. Your confidence and incentives are high but you also know you'll run into trouble every Friday after work when you usually go out with friends, many who smoke. Bow out of that situation for a month. Be honest with your friends and tell them why. Most, if not all of them, will be in support of your goal, and later on when you have successfully quit smoking, you can decide whether or not to join your friends on those Friday nights out. Be aware that when you return to these situations—even when you have successfully replaced an old habit—you will most likely trigger an impulse for that behavior, thus proving there is some truth in the saying that old habits die hard.

Failure can lead to success:
As long as you keep trying, that is. If you fail or experience a setback, pause to reflect truthfully on the reasons for it, figure out what you can do to prevent a similar occurrence in the future, and start again. Never let failure or feelings of guilt keep you from making another attempt. Do not allow yourself to dwell on failure. Remember Thomas Edison, who saw failure as just a way to learn how *not* to do something. Give your mistakes their rightful minute of consideration and then let them go. You have the ability and the know-how to accomplish wonderful things including any goal you set out to achieve. What are you waiting for? Step up to the challenge and soar!

APPENDIX

References and Further Reading

7 Secrets to Success of Steve Jobs. (Undated). YouTube, online.

Agnes, Michael, Ed. 2010. *Webster's New World Collegiate Dictionary, Fourth Edition.* Wiley Publishing.

Alexander. 2013. *Why You Never Forget How to Ride a Bike?* Brain Lagoon, online.

Chomsky, Noam. 2006. *Language and Mind.* Cambridge University Press.

Creative Visualization. March, 2012. Wikipedia, online.

Duhigg, Charles. 2014. *The Power of Habit: Why We Do What We Do in Life and Business.* Random House Trade Paperbacks, New York.

Diamond, Jared. 2006. *The Third Chimpanzee: The Evolution and Future of the Human Animal.* Harper Perennial, New York.

Elrod, Hal. 2012. *The Miracle Morning: The Not-So-Obvious Secret Guaranteed to Transform Your Life (Before 8 AM).* Hal Elrod International, Inc.

Four Minute Mile. November, 2014. Wikipedia, online.

Heath, Chip and Dan Heath. 2010. *Switch. How to Change Things When Change is Hard.* Crown Publishing Group, New York.

Hertzfeld, Andy. February, 1981.*Reality Distortion Field.* Folklore.org

Hill, Napoleon. 1960. *Think and Grow Rich (Revised Edition.)* Fawcett Books, New York.

Hirschfield, Jerry. 1975. *The 12 Steps for Everyone: Who Really Wants Them?* Hazelden, Center City, MI.

Jeffers, Susan. 1987. *Feel the Fear ... and Do It Anyway.* Random House, New York.

Maxwell, John C. 2003. *Attitude 101: What Every Leader Needs to Know.* Thomas Nelson.

Peale, Dr. Norman Vincent. 2003 (1952). *The Power of Positive Thinking.* Fireside, New York.

Pink, David H. 2012. *To Sell is Human: The Surprising Truth about Moving Others.* Riverbend Books/Penguin, New York.

Poertner, Shirley. (No date.) *Jim Carrey's Dream.* iowabiz.com

Wattles, Wallace D. 2009 (1910). *The Science of Getting Rich.* Soil and Health, online.

Online Resources
Alcoholics Anonymous (AA)
http://www.aa.org
Online services include help with finding a local chapter, access to educational video and audio recordings, books in print and in eBook format, self-help tools, and a link to Daily Inspirations.

Al-anon
http://www.al-anon.org
Provides group support and referrals for friends and family of problem drinkers.

Narcanon (Narcotics Anonymous)
http://www.narcanon.org
toll-free hotline: (800) 775-8750
For those struggling with a substance addiction, get help finding a local chapter and referrals, and to read stories of recovery.

YouTube
http://www.youtube.com
Free searchable website containing a vast database of educational videos in addition to popular music and entertainment.

Amazon.com
http://www.amazon.com
World-famous online bookseller that carries both new and used print books, and e-books for instant downloaded to any Kindle device or app. The app is usually free. Amazon also has hundreds of free and nearly free e-books. (Amazon has grown out of the book market and are now purveyors of just about anything you can imagine.)

Two Simple Action Plans

The following sample plans are meant to show you how simple an action plan can be while staying effective. Your action plan should not require an advanced degree in statistics. Keep it simple and have no fear. Tip: When writing your goals and plans, try to use positive phrasing even if the thing you are writing about is a negative. You'll be more receptive later on when you go back to read what you've written today. For example, instead of "I will stop being late for work," consider the more positive "I will arrive on time each workday." Small change - big impact.

1. Single Sentence Plan for a Simple Habit

I will wake up 30 minutes earlier on work days and use this time to have a healthy breakfast so I'll have more energy during the day.

2. One Page Action Plan For A New Habit

The Goal: Get to work on time every day.

Assessment: I waste time in the morning trying on outfits and looking for my keys, and this causes me to be late for work. I will practice getting in the habit of preparing for work the night before.

Reasons to make the change: When I get to work on time, I get to finish on time, and this means I get home earlier and have time to help my kids do their homework or play a game. It helps me be a better parent.

Action Plan: Every night before the next workday...
- Check the alarm clock.
- Decide what to wear.
- Put work clothes on bedroom chair (to avoid opening the closet!)
- Put car keys and notebook on entry table.
- Make sure there is gas in the car.
- Be sure the cat has fresh water and food.
- 5 minutes before bed to visualize arriving on time
- Affirmation is "I arrive on time for work."

Notable Quotes

A cucumber is bitter. Throw it away. There are briars in the road. Turn aside from them. This is enough. Do not add, "And why were such things made in the world?
— *Marcus Aurelius*

Keeping it simple is a gift, a discipline ... complicating it is coming up with a pre-meditated excuse so you don't actually have to do it!
— *Rick Berube*

Life is not for sissies!
— *Rick Berube*

My life didn't please me...so I created a new life.
— *Coco Chanel*

Nothing in life is to be feared. It is only to be understood.
— *Marie Curie*

It had long since come to my attention that accomplished people rarely sat back and let things happen to them. They went out and happened to things.
— *Leonardo Da Vinci*

Your net worth to the world is usually determined by what remains after your bad habits are subtracted from your good ones.
— *Benjamin Franklin*

Man often becomes what he believes himself to be. If I keep on saying to myself that I cannot do a certain thing, it is possible that I may end by

*really becoming incapable of doing it. On the
contrary, if I have the belief that I can do it, I shall
surely acquire the capacity to do it even if I may
not have it at the beginning.*
— *Mahatma Gandhi*

*We can do anything we want to do if we stick to it
long enough.*
— *Helen Keller*

Fail seven times. Stand up eight.
— *Japanese proverb*

*I think one's feelings waste themselves in words;
they ought all to be distilled into actions which
bring results.*
— *Florence Nightingale*

*You wouldn't worry so much about what others
think of you if you realized how seldom they do.*
— *Eleanor Roosevelt*

It wasn't raining when Noah built the ark.
— *Howard Ruff*

*Learn from the past, set vivid, detailed goals for
the future, and live in the only moment of time for
which you have control: now.*
— *Denis Waitley*

Habit Change Cheat Sheet

The way to get started is to quit talking and start doing.
— *Walt Disney*

1. Take responsibility for your life. This means responsibility for where you are now, where you want to be, and what you need to do to get there.
2. Embrace the process. Focus on progress, not perfection.
3. Keep it simple. One day at a time will maximize your potential and transform your potential into the results you want.
4. Have a clear statement of what you want to change and why.
5. Put your action plan in writing. This becomes the contract you make with yourself.
6. Choose a start date. Allow yourself time to prepare for success.
7. Identify your obstacles. This includes people who might not want you to change!
8. Face your obstacles fearlessly.
9. Ask for help when you need it. Have a group of trusted friends, family, co-workers, or clergy who know and support your goal.
10. When mistakes happen, learn and let go. Keep moving forward.
11. Practice every day. Habits are the result of repetition over time.
12. Stay motivated and positive. Use proven behavioral tools such as daily affirmations, inspirational readings, and creative visualization.
13. Be patient. Habits take 30 to 90 days to form, a year or more to become fully ingrained.

Notes...

About the author...

Rick Berube began a career in real estate at the age of 19. He has been coaching agents one-on-one and speaking at training seminars and events throughout North America and Italy for 30 years, using his knowledge and enthusiasm to help others achieve their highest potential.

You can write to Rick via email at

SuccessIsAVerb.com@gmail.com

Made in the USA
San Bernardino, CA
26 January 2018